THE M. & E. HANDBOOK SERIES

BASIC
SOCIOLOGY

F. J. WRIGHT

M.Sc. (Econ.), B.Com. (Lond.), Dip. Ed. (Oxon.)

SECOND EDITION

MACDONALD & EVANS LTD
8 John Street, London WC1N 2HY
1973

First published June 1970
Second impression April 1971
Third impression March 1972
Second Edition September 1973

©

MACDONALD AND EVANS LIMITED
1973

ISBN: 0 7121 0237 X

*Printed in Great Britain by Unwin Brothers Limited, The Gresham Press,
Old Woking, Surrey, England*

AUTHOR'S PREFACE

THESE study notes are intended to introduce to students of social and political affairs, including candidates for the Associated Examining Board's papers in Sociology at Ordinary and Advanced Level, and for the examinations in Social Structure and Sociology for the Ordinary National Certificate in Public Administration, the basic concepts and features of that field of study discussed and argued about as "sociology."

Such a vast amount has been written about the nature and methods of sociology and of the social sciences generally that the beginner is faced with a bewildering succession of theories and suggested approaches and results of investigations in this or that field; he may wonder whether there is such a *discipline* as sociology at all, or whether sociology is merely a conglomeration of all those theories and approaches and reports of investigations. Books with titles like *Sociology* or *An Introduction to Sociology* or *A Textbook of Sociology* may well prove to be dissimilar in their Tables of Contents and diverse in the aspects the author elects to discuss. The author of this HANDBOOK, in offering a work entitled *Basic Sociology*, is conscious that he may be venturing to step where archangels fear to tread. Nevertheless the author has undertaken the work in the belief that some such attempt should be made to indicate and define the essentials of what is still in the eyes of some people a suspect subject, and to assist the student who is honestly wrestling with it as an academic discipline with an examination to face.

Recommended method of study. This book cannot, of course, be used alone as a convenient, prepared notebook dispensing with the necessity of consulting other books on sociology in general and on certain definite fields of study in particular. It is intended to be an *outline guide*, yet one which will stimulate thought, at least curiosity and perhaps enthusiasm, so that the reader is inspired to investigate more closely the various aspects of the field by consulting the works mentioned in the text and in the Bibliography, by reading articles in such journals as *The Listener* and *The Spectator*, by watching television documentaries and listening to radio broadcasts and by reading critically news commentaries in the newspapers. Nearly everybody considers himself to be a sociologist—and often he is not far wrong. However, it is well for the serious student to observe the disciplinary part of the study and a good plan for using this **HANDBOOK** would be as follows:

(*a*) *Read the book through* to get an overall picture of its scope and content, with an eye on the Contents from time to time to note how the subject is treated and to note the major headings.

(*b*) *Then work carefully through the book*, chapter by chapter, testing progress by attempting mentally to answer the questions in the Progress Tests.

(*c*) Read the book again, this time *with special reference to topics* in which one is particularly interested or which are subjects of current discussion in the press or on radio or television, consulting the major works on that subject and acquiring the facts and a confidence in dealing with them, and then *reach a conclusion* which is the result of informed study, however much it may differ from that of an "authority" who is, after all, like everybody else, human.

The student will then realise that sociology is not a soft option but, properly pursued, worthy of his intelligence and serious effort. He will then be able to tackle the Test Paper in Appendix III with understanding and confidence.

April, 1970   **F.J.W.**

PREFACE TO SECOND EDITION

The basic text of the book has remained unchanged in this second edition but it is necessary for works of this kind to be as up to date as possible. Accordingly, the most recently available statistical information has been incorporated, and the nature and effects of recent legislation bearing on the subject matter have been indicated.

In its revised form, therefore, the book should be an even more valuable guide to the facts and theories forming the basis of examinations in sociology. With the practical implications of sociology impinging more and more on the fields of such studies as social structure, the social services and political theory, a grasp of "basic" sociology becomes more and more essential to the students of these fields. Such a basic sociology this **HANDBOOK** aims to provide.

June, 1973.   F. J. W.

NOTICE TO LECTURERS

Many lecturers are now using **HANDBOOKS** as working texts to save time otherwise wasted by students in protracted note-taking. The purpose of the series is to meet practical teaching requirements as far as possible, and lecturers are cordially invited to forward comments or criticisms to the publishers for consideration.

P. W. D. REDMOND
General Editor

CONTENTS

THE NATURE AND DEVELOPMENT OF SOCIOLOGY AS A SCIENCE

PART ONE

THE NATURE AND DEVELOPMENT OF
SOCIOLOGY AS A SCIENCE

CHAPTER I

WHAT IS SOCIOLOGY?

BASIC TERMS

1. The need for definition. To define what we are going to study before we begin is a rule which must be followed in the application of scientific method—the observation of facts, the deduction from the facts, the formulation of hypotheses, and the checking and verification of those hypotheses by the observation and comparison of further facts which may have emerged since the preliminary hypothesis was made. The rule also applies, or should apply, to those studies which comprise the "social sciences"—sciences such as economics and politics, which deal with people living in societies.

2. A tentative definition of sociology. One may suggest that *sociology* is the study of the relationships existing between people living together in communities; it tries to discern patterns in those relationships which may justify the formulation of generalisations about them.

(*a*) For example, one such generalisation is that a community in general is in a state of crisis or decay when the patterns of relationships indicate that the energy, the intelligence, the will to live, the pursuit of cultural achievements, the discipline of government and the moral standards, are such as to indicate that under the pressure of competing communities the fabric of society will collapse and the community will dissolve, just as a business may collapse in competition with a more efficient undertaking. Hindsight has enabled us to see what happened to Classical Greece and Rome.

(*b*) Alternatively a study of a *particular pattern* of relationships may be studied with reference either to one community or to several communities. Emile Durkheim, in his *Du suicide* (1897), studied suicide rates, and he suggested why suicide rates would be lower among Roman Catholics than among Protestants. (*See also* VI, **13.**).

(*c*) In a study such as one of class mobility in relation to educational opportunities, one meets the difficulty of defining "social class," a concept which is somewhat vague. Therefore, some *general acceptance of the concepts* used is necessary if the methods of study, the course of the investigation and the conclusions are to be accepted as valid. However, the *terms of the concepts* may change rapidly in time, as in the case of social class and educational opportunities, so that the value of the investigation becomes mainly historical.

3. A community. The definition of sociology which has been offered has used the term "community," and it is necessary to define this term before going further. A *community* is here defined as a group of people living a common life, observing common customs and a code of general behaviour, with a background of common tradition, subject to a rule or structure of government which is accepted by all. One may speak, for example, of the British community.

(*a*) Such a group commonly inhabit a *territorial area* spoken of as their country, but members of an original group may live somewhere else and yet form a community. Where groups of Jews lived together before the formation of the Israeli state they formed communities of their own, and English people who retire to a kinder climate abroad tend to form little communities in the countries which have granted them rights of residence.

(*b*) It is only in times of war or other crises that there is a *consciousness* of belonging to a community. Where there is no call for general concern or action, the "community" may be little more than a convenient, sociological generalisation (*see also* II, **14**(*a*) and (*b*) and VII, **2**).

NOTE: A phrase such as "the welfare of the community" needs very careful analysis if it is to have definite meaning.

4. A nation. Where there is a consciousness of belonging to a community, with a common history extending back, say, some hundreds of years, or some considerable period, a common pride in the achievements of the group, a common desire to continue the existence of the group and to enhance its prestige, wealth and power, and there is a commonly agreed form of government, then the community is termed a *nation*.

(*a*) A *common language* is not an essential feature of a nation, though there may be an official language, used for official purposes.

(*i*) In Switzerland, for instance, four languages are in use, French, German, Italian and Romansch, three predominantly, with German as the official language.

(*ii*) In Belgium and in Canada two languages are spoken.

(*b*) *Uniformity of race*, or "national characteristics," is not an essential feature for the formation of a nation.

(*i*) In Switzerland there are three "kinds" of Swiss: the French-speaking, Italian-speaking and German-speaking.

(*ii*) The "British" comprise English, Welsh and Scottish peoples, with a mixture of one or two others, according to the migratory flow of peoples, *e.g.* in East Anglia.

(*c*) Occupation of a *specific territory* is not an essential element; the Jews were a "nation" long before the modern state of Israel was created as their homeland.

5. A society. It is necessary to distinguish between a community and a society. A *society* is the complex or totality of the relationships existing between people living in a community—relationships such as marriage and the family unit, the sharing of ethical ideas as to what is right or wrong conduct, and political and religious relationships.

(*a*) A member of a community may be at the same time a father of a family, or a member of a political body, a church or a bowling club.

(*b*) It is the strands of these *relationships* which constitute "society." Groups form communities within a wider community in which, most often, the state plays a dominating role as the arbiter of the life of the community. Given the conditions stated in **4**, a society becomes synonymous with a nation; the existing relationships are recognised as such, and, in a stable society, are generally approved (*see also* VII, **6**).

6. The word "social." This relates to the *taking part* in the life of a society, to the observance of its general rules as well as its laws, and it ranges from the observance of etiquette to conformity with the marriage laws.

(a) The term "social" is, of course, to be distinguished from "sociable": a gangster may be "the life and soul of the party," but his activities are antisocial.

(b) The term "social" may also mean *endeavouring to further*, and not merely maintain, the welfare of society: a lone worker researching into a cure for cancer, as Sir Ronald Ross researched into the problem of malaria, is pursuing a highly "social" activity.

(c) The term "social worker" has a special significance: a *social worker* is a person with a specific function to perform in the field of the social services, *e.g.* a children's officer of a local authority, an almoner or a voluntary welfare worker.

THE STUDY OF SOCIETY

7. Sociology as the "science of society." The significance of the description of sociology as the science of society should now be apparent.

(a) It is, first, the study of the relationships existing in any given community so that *facts* relating to those relationships may be discerned; *e.g.* the customs and laws relating to marriage and the family, the class structure or the moral ideas.

(b) The facts are classified and examined to see if *generalisations* about them are possible; *e.g.* that the social classes in the community appear to be related to occupation or income.

(c) Sociology tries to discern whether *tendencies* or *trends* appear; *e.g.* whether the emphasis in the general conception of the social classes is changing.

(d) Sociology constantly searches for new facts so that the description of the pattern is *checked* and, if necessary, *modified*. The forecasts of population which have been made for Britain have frequently been found to be wrong and the formulation of tendencies based on these predictions must therefore be revised; *e.g.* the Beveridge Report of 1942 advocated children's allowances in the belief that there was a danger of a serious drop in population; in *Social Insurance and Allied Services* (Cmnd. 6404), para. 413, we read that "With its present rate of reproduction, the British race cannot continue; means of reversing the recent course of the birth rate must be found."

8. The difficulties of sociological study. Some of the difficulties of scientific study in sociology, as contrasted with those of the natural sciences like physics and chemistry, are as follows:

(a) The *field of observation and scope of study* in such matters as customs and ways of life are enormous.   Even in the study of primitive or so-called "simple" peoples the investigator finds that the facts relating to the life of the society as a whole and their interpretation (*e.g.* marriage customs, the tracing of lines of descent, the organisation of methods of administering justice) are such that he can spend years researching into and weighing the evidence, *e.g.* Bronislaw Malinowski and his studies of the Trobrianders.

(b) The scope for the *human element* as a factor invalidating one's conclusions is also very great.

(i) The ascertainment of the facts themselves is apt to be coloured by inaccuracy of observation and personal prejudice; *e.g.* witnesses to a motor accident or other occurrence may give different accounts according to whether or not they are sympathetic to the participants.

(ii) The sociologist himself is the product of his own environment, upbringing, tradition, education, heredity and biological constitution.   This is particularly important in matters of morality and religion, in subjects relating to the philosophic conception of the fundamentals, the True, the Good and the Beautiful.   He may "lean over backwards," trying to be dispassionate or disinterested.   A man who batters an old woman to death is a thug who is dangerous to society; he may be "sick," but no amount of reasoning can gloss over his thuggery, which has an immediate impact on society and which has to be dealt with as a *sociological fact,* if other old women are not to be battered to death before the sociologist can reach long-term conclusions about curing the sickness.

9. The dangers of generalisation. We live by generalisations; *e.g.* that certain roads are dangerous to cross at certain times, that we must arrange our finances in a certain way if we are to avoid perennial shortages of cash at, say, Christmas or holiday time.   We cannot bring into our calculations the possibility of winning a big Premium Bond prize.

(a) In dealing with social matters one must *avoid too facile generalisations*; economists have for long realised that it is dangerous to assume that consumers in general act rationally (advertisers have seen to that), and producers often dictate to consumers, not *vice versa*.

(b) Economists, if they are to arrive at any conclusions at all, have to make certain assumptions, *e.g.* that consumers in general will act rationally.   They are aware of these *assumptions*, and qualify their conclusions accordingly.   In sociology there is a danger that one may not recognise assumptions which are really prejudices or unjustified, previously formed conclusions in disguise.   These assumptions are expressed in such dogmatic statements as "Germans are arrogant," or "The lower classes are a rude lot."   Expressed as an art form, a generalisation has implications which go far deeper than personal opinion and it is transformed into a developed thesis giving pleasure and amusement, *e.g.* Mozart's opera *Così fan tutte* (All women are like that). The exceptions are irrelevant.

(c) The search for tendencies and trends may lead one into *devious channels of reasoning and example-seeking* to arrive at a "tendency" which either does not really exist or which can be deduced from common observation and with the aid of common sense.

10. The qualifications of the sociologist.   It would seem that the minimum qualifications of anyone who would describe himself as a "sociologist," with authority to pronounce on human affairs, would be to have lived at least fifty years or so, preferably with a fair amount of personal suffering in his experience; to have a deep and extensive knowledge of such social subjects as economics and politics and the law as well as of the physical sciences, and to be well versed in the arts and music; to have travelled extensively and have some knowledge of the customs, laws and languages of other lands; and to have the ability to observe accurately and draw conclusions supported by adequate proof.

(a) The number of persons possessing such qualifications must necessarily be small; Plato (*see* II, **2** (*a*)) realised that his guardians were not likely to be encountered in this world.

(*b*) The most highly qualified people cannot escape the limitations noted in **8** (*b*).

(*c*) Modern sociologists avoid the world-encompassing surveys of the "Classical" writers, and tend to confine their attentions to the study of a particular field.

(*i*) They may study a *certain area* or refer to a *particular group*: for example, M. Young and P. Willmott in *Family and Kinship in East London* (Routledge and Kegan Paul, 1957) traced the lines of relationship in three generations in a typical working-class household, an extended family with "Mum" standing in a close relationship to her married daughters (*see also* VIII, **8**).

(*ii*) Alternatively, a particular *phenomenon* may be studied with reference to its incidence, causes and implications, *e.g.* suicide (*see* **2**(*b*)).

(*d*) This consideration does enable us to see how, without the equipment of talents and abilities set out above, and without presuming to describe himself as a "sociologist," the ordinary student can learn something about the theories and methods of sociology, and even take part in investigations which will enable him to see his environment in a better light and, as far as is possible in this human world, without prejudice.

PROGRESS TEST 1

1. What is "scientific method"?   (**1**)
2. Define "sociology."   (**2**)
3. What kinds of relationships are discussed in sociology? (**2, 5**)
4. Indicate the difficulties of definition encountered in sociology. (**2**)
5. What is a "community"?   What are the characteristics of a community?   (**3**)
6. What is a "nation"?   What commonly observed features of peoples are not essential in the formation of a nation?   (**4**)
7. Define the terms "society" and "social."   (**5, 6**)
8. What is meant by saying that sociology is the *science of society*?   (**7**)
9. What are some of the difficulties of sociological study?   (**8**)
10. Outline the dangers to be encountered in forming generalisations in sociology.   (**9**)
11. What would be the qualifications of an "ideal" or "expert" sociologist?   (**10**)

CHAPTER II

THE BEGINNINGS OF SOCIOLOGY

POLITICAL PHILOSOPHY

1. The first philosophers. A review of what the keenest thinkers have said about society, or about their own societies, is necessary in order to place sociology, as a study, in perspective. The story begins with *philosophy*, a term which has not yet been adequately defined (*see* V, **4**), but which means basically the study which seeks to place man and his works in relation to the universe—a formidable task. The Greek philosophers were the first people to think about society as a whole, apart, that is, from being in it and taking part in its events, as Spartacus did when he led the revolt of the slaves in 73 B.C. The educated man, wrote Plato, was the man who saw things "whole," *i.e. in perspective*. The Greek philosophers thought about ideas like "justice" and "virtue," having the leisure and the environment to do so. Socrates (469–399 B.C.), whose dialogues were reported by Plato, infuriated his contemporaries by questioning the bases of their beliefs and prejudices.

2. The Greeks. Thus the study of societies in general began with the ancient Greeks, who were greatly concerned with the relationship between man and the state, *i.e.* the Greek city-state. (The word "politics" is derived from *polis*, the Greek city-state.)

(*a*) *Plato* (427–347 B.C.) set out his ideas about an ideal state in three works, *The Republic*, *The Statesman* and *The Laws*.

(*i*) In *The Republic*, he spoke of the well-ordered state where the "just" man was the man who accepted his place in the hierarchy of the three great classes—the guardians or counsellors, the warriors or defenders and the workers or producers of wealth.

10

(*ii*) In *The Statesman*, he made more practicable suggestions about the rule of the philosopher-kings in his communistically organised society.

(*iii*) In *The Laws*, he recognised that more practicable means, such as the separation of powers (*see* 13), are necessary for the running of a community of imperfect people.

(*b*)   *Aristotle* (384–322 B.C.) in his political writings was more of a sociologist than a philosopher.   He traced the evolution of the state from the family group, through the village community, to the city; he classified states into various categories, *e.g.* aristocracies and monarchies.

The Greek city-states failed to survive.   Among the causes of their decay and destruction were wars, internal corruption, slavery and invasion.

3. The Romans. The Romans were more practically minded but less inspired than the Greeks and were greatly concerned with law and order.   Once again, slavery vitiated their conceptions.   The largely Roman philosophy of Stoicism was an austere and demanding creed, cosmopolitan in outlook; and the idea of the narrow city-state was transcended by the idea of the state as a part, not the whole, of life: among its finest exponents were *Seneca* (3 B.C.–A.D. 65) and the emperor *Marcus Aurelius* (A.D. 121–180).

4. The early Christians.   There was much discussion by the early Christian philosophers on the respective spheres of Church and state.   *St Augustine* (354–430), for example, emphasised the distinction between the City of God and the earthly empire or community.

5. Medieval theorists. The distinction between the functions of Church and state continued to be discussed by such thinkers as *St Thomas Aquinas* (1227–74) and *Marsilius of Padua* (1278–1343).   The latter, particularly, was a modernist thinker who would have nothing to do with the medieval idea of the Holy Roman Empire, and spoke of the authority of both Church and state as being derived from the people.

THE RENAISSANCE AND MACHIAVELLIANISM

6. The Renaissance.   The early Renaissance of the fourteenth and fifteenth centuries was the revival of Greek and

Roman culture. It affected men's minds so that the questionings of Marsilius culminated in the debates of the sixteenth-century religious controversialists like Martin Luther (1483–1546) and John Calvin (1509–1564); in political thinking, it inspired the ideas of Machiavelli (*see* **8** and **9**).

The Renaissance was, however, more than a mere revival of Greek and Latin learning: it was a freeing of men's minds from the tyranny of feudalism and the mental subjection to the authority of Church and state; it involved the breaking of Arabian culture upon the narrow rigidities of medieval European thought and the flowing of a tide of appreciation of the Absolutes of Truth, Beauty and Goodness. The Renaissance found its first expression in Italy, where the wealthy cities were able to indulge the taste for art and beauty which accompanied their rising standard of living.

7. The features of the Renaissance. The characteristics of the Renaissance were as follows:

(*a*) The spread of the classical learning and philosophy of Greece and Rome.

(*b*) The *blossoming of the human spirit* in art, literature and scientific enquiry. Leonardo da Vinci (1452–1519) was the exemplar of all-round genius, and the great painters, artists and writers included Michelangelo, Raphael, Titian and Benvenuto Cellini in Italy, the Van Eycks, Dürer and Holbein in Flanders, Holland and Germany, and Shakespeare and Marlowe in England.

(*c*) The *rejection of the authority of the Church in scientific matters*, and the pursuit of scientific enquiry and investigation, *e.g.* the work of Galileo Galilei (1564–1642), which culminated in the application of the principles of physical science to the problems of modern technology.

(*d*) The *revolt against the dogmatism and abuses of the Roman Catholic Church*, which culminated in the Protestantism of Martin Luther and John Calvin. The Reformation provoked a Counter-Reformation on the part of the Catholic Church, and the Jesuits resisted the pretensions to the divine authority of princes on the part of the Protestant rulers.

(*e*) *Geographical exploration*, which eventually opened up new areas of the world for exploitation by commercial companies, which in their turn laid the foundations of empires. Physical and mental expansion made for the decay of feudalism and the rise of great trading organisations, regulated by strong monarchies, and for the rise of national states no longer bound to each other by the idea of a common Christendom.

8. Machiavelli. A figure who has fascinated political philosophers for centuries and who has been the centre of mixed admiration and abuse is Niccolò Machiavelli (1469–1527). He was a Florentine, employed by the Republic (not a republic in the modern sense of the word) on missions to Cesare Borgia and other political leaders, to secure the survival of Florence. In 1512 Florence fell to the Medici family, and Machiavelli was banished, imprisoned, tortured, and finally released, when he retired and wrote his works *The Prince*, *The Art of War* and *Discourses on Livy*, which have infuriated and provoked controversy amongst political thinkers ever since. Machiavelli was not a political philosopher or an academic theorist but a practical man engaged in conducting difficult and dangerous negotiations with colourful, but unscrupulous and violent, personalities. Apart from his personal aim to regain his position with the Medici (hence *The Prince*), he was concerned with specific political and social ends—the unification of Italy from the welter of princedoms and dukedoms tearing it apart, the formation of defence forces (a kind of militia or Home Guard) which would preserve that unity against foreign aggression, and the establishment of peace and prosperity within its frontiers.

9. Machiavellian sociology. If sociology is concerned with arriving (from an examination of existing data relating to the life of a society) at general conclusions on the organisation of that society, and the formulating of policies as to ends and means, then Machiavelli was a sociologist.

(*a*) Machiavelli found that the causes of the poor condition of Italy, marked by corrupt administration and warring factions, were its *lack of unity*, its *lack of order* and the absence of a *strong central government*, its *defencelessness* against foreign foes and its consequent *invasion and devastation* by those foreigners.

(*b*) He thought that if the people *as a whole* were pure in spirit, patriotic and uncorrupted—as he imagined they were

in the great days of the Roman Republic—then a satis-
factory republican state would be achieved. In this his ideas
are applicable to a modern democratic society: the kind of
government a democracy has and the kind of society it
achieves depend on the *character of the people*. Football
hooliganism and "student" riots in a modern community
bear some resemblance to the gladiatorial games riots and
the bread and circuses disturbances of imperial Rome.

(c) Where, however, there are corruption and internal
factions, a dictatorship is the only method of achieving a
strong state; this dictator must be *ruthless and amoral*—a
Prince. One may at least point to the element of strength
in the de Gaulle era in France. Naturally enough, such
ideas provoke a violent reaction from supporters of democracy. But Machiavelli *preferred a democratic republic* to a
dictatorship and honest dealing to a merciless and unscrupulous autocracy. He is abused principally for his
thesis that the end justifies the means, *i.e.* Cesare Borgia was
preferable to anarchy and indiscriminate murder.

(d) Machiavelli's sociology was essentially practical.
Though *he divorced politics from ethics*, his suggested remedy
would have been effective, at least as a short-term measure.
The way in which Italy was subsequently unified, with the
proclamation of the kingdom of Italy in 1861 under Victor
Emmanuel II, does not suggest that Machiavelli's aims could
have been achieved by philosophical argument alone.

NOTE: The experience of Gaullism in France and of Fascism
in Italy suggests that in the long run a strong totalitarian
rule can be maintained only by the *acquiescence of the people*.

THE SOCIAL CONTRACT PHILOSOPHY

10. The place of the state in society. The relation of the
state to the members of a community has been a topic of
discussion for hundreds of years and it is still today, especially
since the Socialist administrations in Britain from 1945; there
have been issues of the most practical importance to ordinary
men and women, from trade unionists to those affected by the
impact of the efforts of the Land Commission. As a background to the discussion of the political system in the social
structure of Britain (*see* XIV), a brief review of the ideas of
the major political philosophers will be useful.

11. Thomas Hobbes. Thomas Hobbes (1588–1679) arrived at a conclusion not so very different from that of Machiavelli, and from similar circumstances.

(*a*) Personal experiences during the English Civil War had convinced him that the price of peace and security could hardly be too high in terms of individual freedom. He postulated in his *Leviathan* (1651) the idea of an *irrevocable contract* between citizen and state by which the state was given absolute power in return for securing peace and security. This doctrine of the "social contract" was rejected alike by supporters of the divine right of kings and protagonists of republican rule.

(*b*) Hobbes's conception of the life of man in his *natural state* was that it was "solitary, poor, nasty, brutish, and short."   He was like Machiavelli in his estimation of human nature.

12. John Locke. This somewhat stark view of man as a political being was modified by both Benedict Spinoza (1632–77), a Dutch philosopher, and John Locke.

Locke (1632–1704) wrote *Two Treatises on Civil Government* in which he supported the idea of a social contract, but denied the irrevocability of this contract and the absolute sovereignty of the state.

(*a*) Only those rights necessary for the smooth running of government should be surrendered to the state, which exists for the *protection of the lives, liberty and property* of the citizens.

(*b*) If the state does not perform these functions properly, it should be *changed* for one that does (this is the forerunner to a similar statement in the Preamble to the American Declaration of Independence of 1776).

13. Montesquieu. The Baron de Montesquieu (1689–1755) in his *L'Esprit des lois* (1748) contrasted the autocracy of the French Louis XV with what he described as the *separation of the powers*, legislative, executive and judicial, in the England of George II.   This separation, he argued, was the means by which tyranny was avoided.

14. Jean Jacques Rousseau. Rousseau (1712–78) wrote *Le Contrat social ou principes du droit politique*, which is regarded as one of the greatest contributions to the development of political thought; and his ideas on liberty, equality and fraternity were the philosophic expression of the inarticulate, vague and confused ideas of the common people before the French Revolution.

(*a*) Rousseau reconciled the sovereignty of the state with the individual will into a *general will*.   This general will has coercive power: if somebody does not agree with the general will, he does not know where his best interests lie, and he should be forced to be "free": a thesis akin to that of the doctrinaire Socialist who believes that Socialism is superior to the British Constitution, because he considers that if Socialist proposals conflict with a Constitution which has been established after many years and is agreed upon by responsible Socialists and non-Socialists alike, then the Constitution must be faulty, because it does not embody the *general will*, as conceived by Socialists.

(*b*) The idea of the "general will" has been the subject of much controversy and is now generally rejected by social psychologists (*see also* VII, 2).

(*c*) Rousseau made a valuable contribution to political thought by stressing the importance of *consent* in government and in showing that the people are the ultimate source of political authority.

POLITICAL SOCIOLOGY

15. The development of political sociology.   The controversy relating to the problems of the state and government in a society has been extended, owing much to the writings of such people as de Tocqueville, Pareto, Durkheim, Weber, Graham Wallas and Karl Marx, into discussions about subjects such as leadership, bureaucracy, public opinion, decision-making, the political process, mass media, etc., so that a subdivision or special study of sociology, political sociology, has become established.

16. The French Socialist writers.   After the French Revolution, such writers as the Comte de Saint-Simon (1760–1825), F. C. M. Fourier (1772–1837), P. J. Proudhon (1809–37) and

Louis Blanc (1811–82) discussed the reorganisation of society on Socialist lines.

17. Philosophy, sociology and social reform. Under the impact of ideas of Socialism, social organisation and social reform, there has often been little to choose between calling a discussion "sociology," "philosophy" or "suggestions for the reform of society," and discussion has ranged between academic abstruseness and suggestions for the practical application of ideas.

18. The political sociologists. Those writers who are of particular importance are the following:

(a) *Immanuel Kant* (1724–1804) in his *Philosophy of Law* (1797) examined such terms as "law" and "liberty" and envisaged a moral revolution which would change the nationalism of his day (he tried not to give offence to his Prussian rulers) into a rational political order.

(b) *Edmund Burke* (1729–97), while supporting the revolt of the American colonists, denounced the French revolutionists in his *Reflections on the French Revolution* (1790).

(c) *Thomas Paine* (1737–1809) replied to this denunciation in his *Rights of Man* (1791–92). He spent some time in France, and was nearly executed as an enemy of the Republic.

(d) *Jeremy Bentham* (1748–1832) was a political philosopher who applied scientific method to social problems; he was active in such social reforms as the mitigation of the criminal law, the reform of the poor law and public health legislation.   He was the originator of the phrase "the greatest happiness of the greatest number" as the philosophical and political expression of *Utilitarianism*.

(e) *John Stuart Mill* (1806–73), the product of the rigorous educational process decreed by his father, James Mill, and a disciple of Jeremy Bentham, advocated in his book *On Liberty* (1859) freedom of thought and expression, and discussed the perhaps insoluble problem of democratic government—how to preserve the freedom of action of the individual without interfering with the freedom of others. His *Representative Government* (1861) discussed the virtue of a wide political franchise.

(*f*) *Herbert Spencer* (1820–1903) was unable to reconcile Socialism with liberty, and in *Social Statics* (1851) and *Man Verus the State* (1884) he urged that there should be limitations on the functions and authority of the state (*see also* III, **10** (a)).

(*g*) *Karl Marx* (1818–83), whose real name was Mordechia, was a Jew who studied Hegelian philosophy in Germany and became a revolutionary journalist. He propounded his ideas in *Das Kapital* and these have stirred the imaginations of Communist revolutionaries ever since. The *Communist Manifesto* (1848), drawn up by Marx and his friend Engels, is an earlier work and is a more intelligible statement of the ideal Communist position. His theories of the class war and of the self-destruction of capitalism have hardly been realised in the states of Western Europe, and the "withering away" of the state has not been seen to happen even in the U.S.S.R. (*see also* III, **15**).

(*h*) The works of later writers such as *T. H. Green, H. J. Laski* and *Bertrand Russell* belong more to the realms of political theory or philosophy than to sociology.

PROGRESS TEST 2

1. What is philosophy? **(1)**

2. What is a city-state, and what did Plato and Aristotle say about the rule of city-states? **(2)**

3. What did Stoicism have to say about the role of the state in social life? **(3)**

4. What did the early Christians and the medievalists think about the roles of the state and the Church in society? **(4, 5)**

5. What were the features of the Renaissance? **(6, 7)**

6. How are the ideas of Niccolò Machiavelli related to modern sociological problems? **(8, 9)**

7. Why are discussions about the nature and functions of the state important in sociology? **(10)**

8. What was the essence of Hobbes's theory of the "social contract"? **(11)**

9. How did John Locke modify Hobbes's view? **(12)**

10. What is the doctrine of the "separation of powers" associated with the name of Montesquieu? **(13)**

11. State briefly the nature of Rousseau's contribution to political thought. **(14)**

12. What is political sociology? **(15)**

13. How would you distinguish between sociology, social philosophy and political thought?   (**10, 15–17;** *see also* I, 7 and V, **4, 5)**

14. What is "Utilitarianism"?   (**18** (*d*))

15. Comment on the work of Karl Marx.   (**18** (*g*)

CHAPTER III

AUGUSTE COMTE AND THE DEVELOPMENT OF SOCIOLOGY

THE FATHER OF SOCIOLOGY

1. The birth of sociology. Sociology as a science in its own right, as distinct from social or political philosophy, began with Auguste Comte (1798–1857), who is often referred to as "the father of sociology." He had many of the qualities which have been suggested as those belonging to the ideal sociologist (*see* I, **10**) and he was also well acquainted with the works of the Classical political writers from Plato onwards.

2. Comte and sociology. Comte's work was not merely a contribution to sociology, though whether he invented the basic theory as well as the term, distinguishing the subject-matter of sociology from that of the other social sciences, is disputable. He studied humanity as a whole—humanity living and evolving as a social being, with the parts of the whole interdependent, so that it was susceptible to generalisations *sui generis*, not reducible to the laws of the other social sciences. He is no more to be dismissed as an "old master," or a "founding father," whose work was important in its own day but is not now up to date, than is, say, Beethoven. Even today, it is often difficult to decide whether certain sociological pronouncements belong to the field of economics, social philosophy, or applied psychology, or are merely pious hopes of a brave new world.

COMTE'S THEORIES OF SOCIOLOGY

3. The Law of the Three Stages. Comte suggested that there are three stages of intellectual development in the history of a society.

(*a*) In the *theological or fictive stage*, a natural phenomenon is interpreted in terms of powers exercised by spirits or gods, or is even *power* itself.

(*i*) Such a stage was passed through in Classical times when the Greek and Roman common people worshipped gods and goddesses and credited their intervention in human affairs, as in the Homeric stories. In modern times, astrological deities and the god Luck play a similar part.

(*ii*) Among primitive peoples the conception of *mana* is closely related to the idea of magical power residing in objects or persons, to some extent controllable by man, as the hunting scenes depicted in caves inhabited by our Palaeolithic ancestors would indicate. The unexplained phenomenon of *poltergeists*, associated with power especially attributable to young girls in less civilised societies, lends some support to the idea of the existence of *mana*.

(*b*) The next stage is the *metaphysical or abstract stage*, in which ideas of things or abstractions correspond to reality in the mind of the individual; abstract forces are regarded as producing the effects attributed in the theological stage to gods or supernatural forces. Modern advertising relies to a great extent on the readiness of people to attribute some abstract quality to a product—often suggested, for example, by associating the idea of a pretty girl with the idea of the product.

(*c*) The final stage is the *positivistic or scientific stage*, in which phenomena are explained on scientific principles.

The three stages, or levels, of experience are passed through by the individual in his progression from childhood to maturity, though they can all be present in the human mind, as in human society, at one and the same time; *e.g.* the Germans in their "scientific" age were susceptible to the myths of race and history propounded by Adolf Hitler.

4. Positivistic science. At the apex of the structure of the levels of thought Comte placed sociology, the science in which the powers of the human mind have reached their peak, for then man begins to know himself.

(*a*) Comte thought that *industrialism* was or would be associated with the third or positivistic stage in human development, in contrast to the theological stage associated with militarism and slavery. The application of "positive"

B

science to the affairs of mankind would necessarily result in human progress towards an era of peace, plenty and understanding.

(*i*) It needs very little knowledge of economics and industrial organisation to realise that we are as yet far from the golden age of peace, plenty and understanding.

(*ii*) A little more knowledge, however, of economics and industrial organisation could convince the most sceptical that in Western civilisation at least a golden age is possible.

(*b*) A *positive science* is one which, like economics, deals with facts as they are observed, as opposed to a *normative* science, like ethics, which deals with norms, or standards of behaviour.

(*i*) It is not always easy to separate the two. A form of moral belief or of economic behaviour may be observed as a fact, but such facts are founded on beliefs of "what ought to be."

(*ii*) There is no doubt that sociology has an intimate connection with both ethics and psychology.

5. Comte and positivism. Comte wrote a history of scientific thinking of which sociology was the climax. Sociology, he wrote, is "the positive study of the totality of fundamental laws relating to social phenomena." It is therefore the most complex of the sciences. While being a scientific method, a means, it must also have ends.

(*a*) The distinction between means and ends, and the clear statement of the ends, is not always easily made.

(*b*) *Voir pour prévoir*, to see in order to predict, is the aim that follows from the establishment of laws or tendencies in human society. But one may add that prediction is only of intellectual value if it is based on what has been, because the will of human beings tries to determine what a situation will actually be.

6. Social statics and social dynamics. Comte divided sociology into "static" and "dynamic" sociology.

(*a*) *Social statics* involves the examination of the ways in which social phenomena are connected; *e.g.* one observes the structure of the family at different stages of development and the relationship of the family to other parts of the social structure at these stages.

(b) *Social dynamics* is concerned with progress in human development.   The Law of the Three Stages (*see* 3) is fundamental to this progress.

SOCIOLOGY AFTER COMTE

7. The value of Comte's work to sociological thought.
Though Comte's work may now be regarded as too general in scope and as attempting something which has been and probably always will be too vast and intricate to set out in logical, definite form, he did give a direction to such a study.

(a) His emphasis on the need to study social phenomena *in relation to the conditions in which they occur* is of fundamental importance to social investigation; it gave such investigations a new orientation—they became sociology and not social philosophy.

(b) His *distinction between social statics*, the conditions of the environment of societies, *and social dynamics*, the processes of change in societies, is equally fundamental.

Whatever the arguments, objections and discussions that have centred around his work (which are in themselves evidence of the impact of that work) there is no doubt that Comte occupies a unique place in the development of sociological thought.   The study was to be called *sociology*, a subject distinct from history and political philosophy which had been the field of social philosophers from Plato onwards. From now on there was to be a "science" of society, even though the science was to be only the scientific method used in its study, used to discern the parts of the great whole which is the story of Man.

8. The increasing self-consciousness of social life.   Man was becoming aware of the *fact* of society and its problems as a whole in a much more distinct way than before.   This was due to a number of developments: the technical advances of the Industrial Revolution, and the social consequences of that industrial expansion which social workers and statesmen alike attempted to solve; the progress in biological science and the controversies that resulted when that progress evoked such violent reaction from religious dogmatists; the anthropological work of such investigators as Sir E. B. Tylor, whose *Primitive*

Culture was published in 1871, and Sir James Frazer, whose work *The Golden Bough* (first edition 1890) became part of standard anthropological literature; the revolution in transport and communications; and the organisation of labour in trade unions. All these factors produced a society which was more self-conscious and concerned with group means and ends than society, in a national sense, had been before. As the nineteenth century progressed into the twentieth, this was intensified by the First World War, with its slaughter and hatreds, and the economic depression which came to its culmination in the 1930s and prepared the way for another world war.

9. Sociological study. Several lines of approach to the broad field of social study emerged:

(*a*) Investigators in *special fields* made use of the broad conclusions of other sciences like psychology and ethics to study the culture of primitive societies and gain some insight into the social attitudes generally of such peoples. Thus, *Bronislaw Malinowski* (1884–1942) studied the Melanesians of New Guinea and concluded that elements, customs or instruments of a society are organised around the serving of some definite function, *e.g.* religious or economic, in that society; this kind of approach is known as "functionalism" (*see* **14**).

(*b*) Some investigators studied *special aspects* of society such as suicide (*see* I, 2 (*b*)) or division of labour or capitalism (*see* **11** and **12** (*c*)).

(*c*) *Specific cultures in specific areas* were studied; *e.g.* M. Young and P. Willmott published their findings in *Family and Kinship in East London* (Routledge and Kegan Paul, 1957).

(*d*) *Broad reviews* of social life as a whole, in order to arrive at some thesis about social facts in general, have appealed to certain writers of warm humanity and high intellectual development (*see* **17** and **18**). It is this kind of work which treats sociology as "the positive study of the totality of fundamental laws relating to social phenomena."

THE ORGANIC SCHOOL AND FORMALISM

10. The "organic school." The preoccupation of early sociologists with biology and the work of men such as Charles

III. DEVELOPMENT OF SOCIOLOGY   25

Darwin (1809–82) and Alfred Russel Wallace (1823–1913) on the origin of species and the theory of natural selection led many sociologists to draw comparisons between society and the human organism.   They used terms such as the "organs of society" and "the differentiation of its parts."

(a) An outstanding writer of this kind was *Herbert Spencer* (1820–1903).   He wrote his *Principles of Sociology* in three volumes, taking thirty-three years to fulfil this task. He used evidence from biology and anthropology, and applied his criteria of complexity, differentiation and integration to human society: the differentiation of functions in society and an increasing "positivistic" move towards scientific control of the human environment would result in greater production, more leisure and a greater pursuit of ideals (*see also* II, **18** (*f*)).

(b) Spencer's work had a great influence in America, where W. G. Sumner (1840–1910) used the ideas of "folkways" (social habits and customs) and "mores" (folkways of greater normative power) in justifying a philosophical view of society distinguished by a typically American confidence in the virtues of a competitive, *laissez-faire* and technologically developing society.

11. The "formal school."   Another "school" was based on the idea of the forms of social relationship.

(a) The German *Georg Simmel* (1858–1918) applied the philosophy of Immanuel Kant (1724–1804) to the problem of society and wrote about the *forms* which social relationships take.   He investigated the relation between the individual and the group, and considered such forms of social relationships as competition, subordination and division of labour, which could be studied as forms of relationships occurring in all societies.

(b) *Alfred Vierkandt* (1867–1953) was concerned with the *psychological aspects* of social relationships, *e.g.* the attitudes of respect, shame and submission.   His aim was to describe "irreducible" categories of social relationships in order to arrive at the fundamental forces that induce change.

(c) *Leopold von Wiese* (1876–1961) emphasised the *empirical* approach, *i.e.* one based on observation and experiment. Social relationships, he held, were to be studied without reference to their purposes, a rather barren approach, since social actions can hardly be studied without reference to ends or purposes (*see* **5**).

(*d*) *Max Weber* (1864–1920) pursued the idea of forms or types in social relationships. By categorising *ideal types* we can arrive at a basis of comparison; such ideal types include capitalism and Protestantism. Weber wrote about world religions and bureaucracy on these lines.

FUNCTIONALISM

12. Emile Durkheim. Emile Durkheim (1858–1917) was the pioneer of the "functional school," though his work was of such wide scope and depth that he is regarded as one of the outstanding sociological thinkers of the nineteenth century. He has links with the organic school and with those who regard sociology as the synthesis of the social sciences.

(*a*) He divided sociology into *three divisions*, which are as follows:

(*i*) *Social morphology*, which is concerned with the geographical basis of peoples and its relation to types of social organisation; such problems as the distribution of population would come within its scope.

(*ii*) *Social physiology*, which deals with the various branches of sociology, each concerned with a special set of social facts, *e.g.* morals, law and economics.

(*iii*) *General sociology*, which synthesises the conclusions of the social sciences such as economics and social institutions, in so far as it determines what are *social* facts and seeks to establish whether there are any general laws relating to these facts.

(*b*) The obligations imposed by a society upon individuals, *e.g.* moral observances, led him to the conclusion that *society exists as a being* distinct from the individuals composing a community and is superior to them.

(*c*) Durkheim used *statistical data* to support his thesis of the existence of a social solidarity. *The Division of Labour* and *Suicide* are two of his greatest works showing the application of his ideas (*see* **I**, **2**(b)).

(*d*) The happiness of the individual, he contended, is

assured by *socially approved norms or standards*. In the absence of these, the individual personality suffers a disorganisation—a state he called "anomie" (*see also* IV, **16**).

(*e*) In *The Elementary Forms of Religious Life* he explored the relationship between the individual personality and the social system.

13. Durkheim's influence. Durkheim has had an important influence on French sociology and on the sociology of other writers.

(*a*) *Malinowski* and *Radcliffe-Brown* (*see* IV, **12**) adopted his methods for their "functional" studies in anthropology.

(*b*) *Parsons* (*see* IV, **11**) and *Merton* (*see* IV, **13**) in America have acknowledged their debt to him.

14. Functionalism. Durkheim made more precise the ideas of Herbert Spencer (*see* **10** (*a*)), who first used this term, by emphasising that in order to explain a social phenomenon one must first discover the cause that produces it and then the function that it fulfils in the total social activity.

(*a*) The application of the functional idea in complex industrial societies has proved more difficult than with the more simple peoples.

(*b*) Merton used the terms "function" and "dysfunction" in relation to social change (*see* IV, **13**).

(*c*) The term "function" may well be used in a subjective way and be disputed on "ideological" grounds: *e.g.* social inequality may have a function though the fact itself may be disapproved of by advocates of egalitarianism, who might think of it as a malfunction or failure of function.

ECONOMICS AND SOCIETY

15. Karl Marx. Karl Marx (1818–83) and V. Pareto (1848–1923) (*see* **16**), in common with Weber (*see* **11** (*d*)), attributed considerable importance to the economic aspects of society. Karl Marx (*see also* II, **18** (*g*)) was a social and economic historian and a political propagandist rather than a political sociologist.

(*a*) He took a materialistic view of history, believing that the evolution of societies has been determined by *economic needs*. He preached a theory of the class war, justified by his theory of the "surplus value" which is added to all goods by the labour which produces them.

(*b*) He predicted the collapse of capitalism and the establishment of a *proletarian, classless society*.

(*c*) Though Marx's predictions have not been fulfilled, his formidable work *Das Kapital* and particularly the *Communist Manifesto*, drawn up by Marx and his friend Engels, have had a tremendous effect on political thought throughout the world, and provided a theoretical basis for Lenin in the Russian Revolution.

16. V. Pareto.   Pareto drew a distinction between what is rational and what is believed to be rational, but which is in fact based on faulty logic.

(*a*) He called rationalisations *derivations*, and the reality behind them *residues*.

(*b*) In conceiving such terms as "the persistence of aggregates" to describe conservative ways of thinking and "the circulation of élites," Pareto appears to have fallen into the trap of particular danger to modern sociologists— that of coining words and phrases to denote concepts which either are too difficult to express in precise scientific terms, or are incapable of such expression; they are words and phrases which may express simple ideas in a complex manner.   Sociologists often appear as if they are desperately trying to justify the existence of sociology by inventing a mystique of technology.

SOCIOLOGY IN BRITAIN

17. British sociology.   British sociologists have been more concerned with the application of sociological method to specific aspects or areas of social life than with the discussion of abstract or all-embracing generalisations.   They have discussed such matters as morals, religion and social classes in a spirit of scientific caution rather than inspired enthusiasm.

18. British sociologists.   Sociologists such as Hobhouse and Westermarck were the dominating influences on British sociology before the Second World War.   Their work was permeated with a sense of high purpose and was concerned especially with the ideals of social justice and social development.

(a) The first chair of sociology was founded at the London School of Economics and occupied by L. T. Hobhouse (1864–1929), who was interested particularly in social change and development. Rejecting a biological approach, he applied psychology to the facts of social life in his *Mind in Evolution* (1926), and applied the results of ethics and psychology in his *Morals in Evolution* (1915). With G. C. Wheeler and M. Ginsberg (a later successor to the chair), he pioneered the comparative method in *The Material Culture and Social Institutions of the Simpler Peoples* (1915), correlating the facts of the economic situation, government, justice, marriage customs, status and rank, and property among primitive peoples. Hobhouse came to optimistic conclusions about social development.

(b) *E. A. Westermarck* (1862–1939), a Finn, succeeded Hobhouse at the London School of Economics. He was interested particularly in the comparative study of morals. His work, *The History of Marriage*, became a classic.

(c) *Morris Ginsberg* (1889–1970) followed in their tradition, though he did not attempt a great work on the lines of Spencer, Hobhouse or Westermarck. He pursued a quiet, effective path of the survey of the field and offered constructive criticism of the writers on the subject. In his *Sociology* (1934) and *The Psychology of Society* (1921) he displayed a talent for clear, common-sense exposition and a keen sense of the absurdities of obscurantism and tortuous grappling with ideas, created by the writer and not by the situation. The collected papers of his contribution to social philosophy have been published in three volumes under the general title of *Essays in Sociology and Social Philosophy* (Heinemann, 1947–61). The titles of the volumes are *On the Diversity of Morals*, *Reason and Unreason in Society* and *Evolution and Progress*.

PROGRESS TEST 3

1. Why is August Comte often referred to as "the father of sociology"? **(1, 2)**

2. State and illustrate the Law of the Three Stages.   **(3)**

3. Why did Comte place sociology at the apex of the structure of levels of thought?   **(4)**

4. What is a "positive" science?   **(4** (*b*)**)**

5. Why is sociology "the positive study of the totality of fundamental laws relating to social phenomena"?   **(5)**

6. Define and illustrate "social statics" and "social dynamics."   **(6)**

7. Give a brief estimate of the value of Comte's work to sociology, and show how he gave a direction to the study of sociology.   **(7)**

8. Why did society become more self-conscious during the nineteenth century and afterwards?   **(8)**

9. What approaches to sociology were made as a result of this greater social awareness?   **(9)**

10. What were the characteristics of the organic school?   **(10)**

11. What was the central basis of investigation of the formal school?   **(11)**

12. Review the contribution to sociology of Emile Durkheim.   **(12, 13)**

13. What is meant by "functionalism"?   **(12–14)**

14. What writers have been influenced by the idea of "functionalism"?   **(13, 14)**

15. Briefly comment on the approach made by (*a*) Karl Marx, (*b*) V. Pareto, in discussing the economic aspects of society.   **(15, 16)**

16. What have been the characteristics of the British school of sociology?   **(17)**

17. Mention some of the contributions made to sociology by L. T. Hobhouse, E. A. Westermarck and Morris Ginsberg.   **(18)**

CHAPTER IV

MODERN SOCIOLOGY

THE REASONS FOR THE DEVELOPMENT OF MODERN SOCIOLOGY

1. The growing interest in sociological problems. This interest is the product of events which have forced the attention of men and women to the problems of their societies as a whole, as distinct from personal or group problems; it has become increasingly recognised that those personal or group problems are aspects, results or concomitants of the wider national or international problems. The sociological problems have indicated the culmination of processes which have affected the personal lives of men and women to an increasing extent.

2. Scientific consolidation. The twentieth century saw the culmination of a period of scientific consolidation, which began with Newton and which has been carried on through the engineering achievements of the present day, with its effects on power, transport, communications, propaganda and the opportunities generally available for the making of material wealth. The social consequences of this industrial expansion, interacting with the inequalities of the control and use of wealth, have been expressed in problems relating to population and its distribution, class structure, the relations between employers and employees, and the political system.

NOTE: The author has written about the social and political consequences of industrial expansion in *The Evolution of Modern Industrial Organisation* Macdonald and Evans, Third Edition, 1967).

3. The scientific method of investigation. This form of investigation of facts, their correlation, the formulation of hypotheses and the application of these hypotheses in social policies, began to be used in the practical work of social philosophers, administrators and social reformers.

(a) The philosopher Jeremy Bentham (see II, 18 (d)) was the first to apply scientific method to social problems.

(b) Other reformers who worked on the social problems of the Industrial Revolution included James Kay (later Sir James Kay-Shuttleworth), who wrote The Moral and Physical Condition of the Working Classes (1832); Edwin Chadwick, whose Report on the Sanitary Condition of the Labouring Population (1842) shocked the well-to-do, ignorant of such problems; Charles Booth, who wrote The Life and Labour of the People in London (1891–1903), and B. Seebohm Rowntree, who made a survey of conditions in York in 1899, entitled Poverty: A Study of Town Life (1901), which he followed later with other studies of poverty.

4. The economic and social situation. The First World War, followed by the inter-war period of confusion, distress and the unemployment which reached its lowest depths in the 1930s, and then the Second World War, accelerated the movement towards the liberalism of the twentieth century, and shocked the nation into a progress which culminated in the Welfare State, and brought sociology into the arena of contemporary life.

The changes in the institutional life of the nation, in the family, in religious and moral ideas, in the impact and treatment of crime, in the nature and mobility of social classes, and in the administration of the activities of the state, have been such as to demand the attention of a sociology which is removed from mere philosophy and which must achieve results of some practical significance to ordinary men and women if it is to command respect as a study at least as relevant to everyday affairs as economics.

5. The academic status of sociology since the Second World War. Since the Second World War there has been a very great increase in the interest shown in sociology in academic circles, and the general public has heard the expression "sociology" uttered more often, and sometimes heard it with scepticism and irritation. Economists had been inclined to look askance at sociology as being a vague, woolly subject with pretensions to being a science, which justified Mark

Twain's gibe: "There is something fascinating about science. One gets such wholesale returns of conjecture out of such a trifling investment of fact" (*Life on the Mississippi*).

(*a*) Since the beginning of the 1960s particularly, the universities have expanded their opportunities for the study of sociology, and sociology now appears as an "O" and "A" Level subject in the examinations of the Associated Examining Board.

(*b*) Besides degrees in general sociology, academic qualifications may be obtained in special fields; *e.g.* in the sociology of education, in which at least one institution to date awards a Mastership.

(*c*) The great expansion in social work and in the facilities for training in it, *e.g.* child care, the probation service, have encouraged a greater interest in sociological subjects.

(*d*) In March 1972, the Post Office advertised appointments for a planner and a sociologist; the sociologist was to be responsible for "*studies into* the behavioural impact of Telecommunications services on people; the likely patterns of social and economic development and their effect on the type, volume and timing of Telecommunications services;" and *evaluating* the implications of the use of time by Business and Residential customers; the part that Telecommunications services can play in society in the long-term future.

MODERN THEORIES OF SOCIOLOGY

6. The search for a sociological theory. Oswald Spengler (1880–1936), a German philosopher, came to the conclusion in his work, *The Decline of the West*, that Western societies were not going forward to new progress, but would reach a climax, decline and die. This pessimistic conclusion has not been welcomed by those who believe that history is not inevitable, that the future is not already printed as on a cinema film, to be rolled off as the story unfolds, but that men, by a study of society, can learn enough about themselves and the societies in which they live to influence the development of those societies. Hence the search for a *theory* of society, a search which has ranged from broad speculations of a psychological nature to the investigations of peoples, classes, social customs and beliefs, so that conclusions will be reached which will be of value in understanding and influencing society.

7. Some notable sociologists.

(a) *Henry Thomas Buckle* followed Spencer (*see* II, **18** (*f*)) in the adoption of the theory of *the inheritance of acquired characteristics*, promulgated by Lamarck (1744–1829), and in his *History of Civilisation in England* (1856) he laid great emphasis on the importance of *environment*, *e.g.* the influence of geography on religion. He held, with Comte, that the discovery of general social laws and the action taken upon them could ensure the happiness and efficiency of society.

(b) *Hobhouse* (*see* III, **18** (*a*)) agreed with Durkheim that the ultimate aim of sociology was to provide a *synthesis of the social sciences* (*see* III, **12**) so that lines of development of societies could be discerned, and in his *Social Development* he tried to discover what criteria of development there were and the conditions under which such development occurs.

(c) *Wilhelm Wundt* (1832–1920) also believed that it was possible to arrive at a *scientific study of society*, and that principles could be discovered linking together such aspects as ethnology and political science and so producing a social philosophy. He was an experimental psychologist as well as a philosopher.

(d) *Graham Wallas* (1858–1932) was one of the founders of the science of *social psychology*; he pointed out the irrationality of the forces behind "public opinion" and politics.

AMERICAN SOCIOLOGY

8. The American influence on sociology. With the coming of the Second World War and the increase of the power of the U.S.A., American sociologists turned with confidence to the classification of societies, tracing the stages by which societies became industrialised and "modern" and examining the hindrances to this "modern" development.

9. Rostow and economic growth. The idea of evolution in society and of the formation of stages in the development from primitive conditions to the culmination of an affluent, mass-consumption society has been pursued by W. Rostow in *The Stages of Economic Growth* (Cambridge University Press, 1960). As a description of the stages leading to the kind of society that now exists in the U.S.A., there appears to be considerable justification for Rostow's classification, though his categories may seem to be descriptions of the obvious. The importance of such developments to the sociologists (and, of course, to the people who compose the societies concerned) lies in the nature and significance of the social changes which accompany economic development.

10. Rostow's stages of economic development. The main stages of evolution are as follows:

(*a*) The first stage is characterised by a *primitive agricultural economy.*

(*b*) The *preconditions of a take-off stage* show an industrial revolution and a centralisation of power within a framework of law and order. This stage occurred in nineteenth-century France and is to be found in the developing countries today.

(*c*) Rostow then speaks of a *take-off stage*, as in Britain, 1783–1802, the U.S.A., 1843–60, Argentina since 1935, and India and China since 1952. It leads to stages four and five. The conception of this stage may perhaps provoke the most criticism of Rostow's scheme, on the grounds that the following stages are a description of what has happened in industrial societies rather than a description of an evolutionary stage.

(*d*) In stage four, the *drive to maturity*, the economic growth is faster than the growth of population, and diversification of industry meets international competition.

(*e*) Stage five is the *high mass-consumption* stage that has been reached in the U.S.A., Canada, Australia and New Zealand, and some countries in Western Europe. The problems of affluence and the production of non-essential and non-durable goods for a mass market, and the necessity for the production of more and more goods if industry is to survive, are solved by the government draining the citizens' incomes on war, space research, intensive industrial propaganda and the production of goods with built-in obsolescence.

NOTE: It is emphasised that, as in all the works mentioned in this book, the work or theory under discussion must itself be read carefully before a judgment can be made on its worth or validity.

11. Talcott Parsons. Talcott Parsons has become known as the prophet of the analysis of evolutionary trends and movements which lead to the emergence of a modern, efficient state like the U.S.A.

(*a*) In 1964 Parsons published his essay *Evolutionary Universals in Society*, a title which in itself indicates the general lines of his thought. Following the principles of "social action analysis," he has classified behaviour on the basis of the motivations of the "social actor" (see T. Parsons, *The Structure of Social Action* (McGraw-Hill, 1937) and T. Parsons and E. Skils, *Toward a General Theory of Action* (Harvard Press, 1951) and *Structure and Process in Modern Societies* (Free Press, 1961)).

(*b*) Parsons also concerned himself with "functional analysis" (*see* III, **14**). He said that four "functional exigencies" had to be met if a social system were to survive. These were the following:

    (*i*) Goal attainment.
    (*ii*) Adaptation.
    (*iii*) Integration.
    (*iv*) Pattern maintenance.

Around these exigencies, or demands, institutions arise and maintain themselves, performing specialised functions, *e.g.* the functions of politicians.

FUNCTIONALISM IN AMERICAN SOCIOLOGY

12. Functionalism and the anthropologists. It was considered by some sociologists that the "functionalism" theory had been tied too much to primitive communities, as in the works of Durkheim, A. Radcliffe-Brown (see his *Structure and Function in Primitive Society* (Cohen and West, 1952)) and B.

Malinowski in his work on the Trobriand Islanders of the South Pacific (see his *Sexual Life of Savages* (Routledge and Kegan Paul, 1929), *Crime and Punishment in Savage Society* (Routledge and Kegan Paul, 1920) and *Argonauts of the Western Pacific* (Routledge and Kegan Paul, 1922)). Theirs was an "organismic" approach, and their conclusions, as to, *e.g.*, the functions of magic in primitive societies, had little application to modern communities.

(*a*) It was objected that the description of the origin and persistence of a sociological element does not explain the *maintenance* of the social system as a whole, as Radcliffe-Brown tried to do.

(*b*) Malinowski concentrated on the origin and persistence of particular elements, *e.g.* magical practices and rituals, without resolving the problem of *persistence* itself.

NOTE: One may suggest here that, as has been observed before in this book, magic exists in modern industrialised societies, in advertising, for instance; advertising performs a function, but this is not to say that its utility justifies its necessity.

13. Robert K. Merton. It has been claimed that the American sociologist, Robert K. Merton, has freed the concept of functionalism from its biological and anthropological traditions (see *Social Theory and Social Structure* (Free Press, 1967)).

(*a*) He classified the consequences of patterned elements or usages or customs into the following:

(*i*) Those which enable the social system to meet internal or external demands; these are called *functions*.

(*ii*) Those which lessen the adaptation or adjustment of the social system; these he called *dysfunctions*.

(*iii*) Those which are *not related* to the adaptation or adjustment.

(*b*) Both functions and dysfunctions may be *manifest*, *i.e.* with recognised and intended consequences, and they may be *latent*, *i.e.* not recognised or intended.

NOTE: These terms are used in a sense opposite to that used by Freudian psychiatrists: the *manifest* content of a dream is its apparent or surface content, whilst the *latent* content is the real, hidden meaning.

(*c*) It is clear that the distinction between function and dysfunction is a useful one especially in dealing with problems of social change, although it is difficult to evaluate in practice; *e.g.* it would be difficult to evaluate the functions and dysfunctions of the introduction of comprehensive education in Britain's secondary education system.

"MIDDLE-RANGE" THEORIES

14. "Middle-range" studies. Merton also examined the function of bureaucratic organisation and the behaviour expected of officials. This type of study is concerned with what Merton called "middle-range" theories—those between the wide-embracing theories of social behaviour and those relating to limited fields, such as specific groups, *e.g.* the work of W. I. Thomas and F. Znaniecki on *The Polish Peasant in Europe and America* (1918).

15. Group theories. A great deal of work has been carried out by the Americans on social groups, *e.g.* Theodore Newcomb's study of Bennington Women's College in the U.S.A. (see his *Social Psychology*, 1953) and S. Staffer's *The American Soldier* (Princeton University Press, 1949). Perhaps the most famous study of this kind is the series of Hawthorne experiments carried out at the Western Electric Company's works between 1929 and 1932 on the "team spirit".

(*a*) Perhaps the distinction between a *reference group*, with which an individual wishes to identify himself, and a *membership* group, of which he is a member but with which he does not wish to identify himself, is a useful one.

(*b*) Those who identify themselves with groups engaging in a certain type of behaviour may not themselves be the best judges of the significance of their behaviour.

16. Deviant behaviour. Behaviour which does not conform to that generally accepted in a group is termed *deviant behaviour*. Merton has concerned himself with explaining variations in rates of deviant behaviour and has tried to discover how social structures can exert a pressure on persons in a society to engage in nonconformist conduct.

(*a*) He used the conception of *anomie*, first used by Durkheim (*see* III, **12** (*d*)), to denote "a breakdown in the cultural structure, occurring particularly where there is an acute disjunction between cultural norms and goals and the socially structured capacities of members of the group to act in accord with them." The society as a whole is unstable, lacking in accepted norms or standards.

(*i*) *Cultural goals* are those objectives and ambitions which the individual is encouraged to pursue by the social structure.

(*ii*) The prescribed ways of pursuing them are called by Merton *institutionalised means*.

(*b*) An individual may accept either or both of these goals and means: *deviance* may occur if, for example, he rejects a goal but pursues the recognised institutionalised means of pursuing it; then the deviance is expressed in *ritualism* (*see also* VII, **5** (*d*)).   If he rejects both the goal and the means and substitutes his own goal and means, this is *rebellion*.

(*c*) Merton suggested that contemporary American society has reached a state of anomie because the stress on a goal such as the accumulation of wealth has been unaccompanied by the possession of legitimate means of achievement.

(*i*) The assassination of Senator Robert F. Kennedy led to the formation of the National Commission on the Causes and Prevention of Violence, which published investigative studies of several civil disorders in the United States in 1968, and which issued the first of several task force reports in 1969. A summary by Hugh Davis Graham and Ted Robert Gurr spoke of "a kind of historical amnesia" masking much of their turbulent past which is the heritage of Americans and of their vision of themselves as "a latter-day chosen people."

(*ii*) Although 220 Americans died in violent civil strife in the five years before mid-1968, the rate of 1·1 per million population was infinitesimal compared with the average of 238 deaths per million for all nations, and it was less than half the European average of 2·4 per million.

(*d*) The state of affairs noted in (*c*) appears to be the state of mankind in general: in simple terms, *delinquency*, for example, may be related to frustration of desire.

17. Conflict.   Society is not an organism of which the parts work harmoniously together: there is conflict in each individual, as Freud and his successors pointed out.   In society, as in the individual, the system may be sufficiently integrated to accept social change without such a stress threatening its reasonably harmonious functioning; *e.g.* the changes brought about by a Labour Government in Britain from 1964–1970, or the reorganisation of a bureaucracy such as that following the Fulton Committee report in 1968. The term *dynamic equilibrium* has been used of this condition.

(*a*) There are, however, *conflicts between the elements of a society* which may seriously threaten its stability; *e.g.* the conflicts between Protestants and Roman Catholics in Northern Ireland which began in 1969, the conflicts between organised labour and the employers in Britain, and conflicts between the trade unions themselves.

(*b*) Though there is nothing in Britain like the "class war" predicted by Karl Marx (*see* II, **18** (*g*)), conflict may result from the *contact of different ways of thought and habits*; *e.g.* when an industrial development results in the immigration of "foreigners" into a community with a hitherto stable structure (see Margaret Stacey, *Tradition and Change: A Study of Banbury*, (Oxford University Press, 1960).

(*c*) Individuals may be *at war* with their society or their group. The sheer weight of the conformity of the group will cause the major disturbance and suffering to fall heavily upon the deviant individual.

(*d*) Lack of knowledge, lack of technological ability, lack of organisational power and *disagreement* between the members of a group as to what constitutes the "good life" will cause the efforts of those trying to express their aspirations for a new world to fail; *e.g.* the student riots and disturbances of the late 1960s. If the disturbances are powerful enough to wreck the structure of society, there will be chaos, anarchy, the rule of force and, eventually, the reaching of an equilibrium very like the old, except in the nature of the political control.

PROGRESS TEST 4

1. What are the reasons for the greater interest shown generally in sociology during the twentieth century? **(1–4)**

2. What changes have taken place in the academic status of sociology generally since the Second World War? **(5)**

3. What writers have sought to find a general theory of society? **(6, 7)**

4. Review the characteristics of the American contribution to sociology. **(8–16)**

5. Describe the characteristics of Rostow's "stages of economic growth." **(9, 10)**

6. What is the importance to the sociologist of the study of industrial expansion? **(9)**

7. Why has Talcott Parsons become known as "the prophet of the analysis of evolutionary trends and movements leading to the emergence of a modern, efficient state"? **(11)**

8. What has been the connection between social anthropology and "functionalism"? **(12)**

9. What contribution did Robert K. Merton make to the "functional" theory? **(13)**

10. What are "functions" and "dysfunctions"? **(13)**

11. What are "middle-range" studies? **(14)**

12. What is (a) a "reference group," (b) a "membership group"? **(15)**

13. What is "deviant" behaviour? **(16)**

14. How did Merton use the term "anomie"? **(16)**

15. Explain: (a) cultural goals; (b) institutionalised means; (c) ritualism; (d) rebellion. **(16)**

16. What conflicts may occur in a society? **(17)**

17. Explain the state of "dynamic equilibrium" in a society. **(17)**

CHAPTER V

THE SOCIAL SCIENCES

SOCIOLOGY AND THE SOCIAL SCIENCES

1. The special social sciences. The nature and scope of sociology as a scientific study have been discussed, and it is now possible to see how sociology differs in its nature and scope from those other studies which, while being concerned with people living in societies, as sociology is, deal with specific aspects of social life, each a discipline of its own, with its own fields and methods of investigation. They are the "special" social sciences, and they are generally held to comprise the following:

(*a*) *Economics* is the study of the ways in which peoples and nations make a living. It is concerned with "house-keeping," from the Greek word of that meaning.

(*b*) *Politics*, or political science, is the study of forms of government, from the Greek word *polis*, the city-state, a word which had a religious as well as a political significance to the Classical Greeks.

(*c*) *Ethics* is the study of standards of conduct, and is more particularly related to what people think is the ideal of the Good Life.

NOTE: Ethics is a *normative* study, dealing with standards or norms of conduct—what people think *ought to be*. Contrasted with normative studies are *positive* studies, concerned with what *is*, *e.g.* economics and politics (*see also* III, **4** (*b*)).

(*d*) *Social psychology* is concerned with the facts of mental experience in the life of societies. It is concerned, *e.g.*, with the thesis that there is a "general will" (*see* II, **14** (*a*) and(*b*)), with crowd behaviour and the phenomenon of leadership.

(*e*) *Social anthropology* is the study of man's place in the animal kingdom, in particular, and how society exists in simple peoples, as expressed in their customs and laws and beliefs (*see* **7** (*d*)

(*f*) *Ethnology* is the study of races.

(*g*) *Law* is the study of the rules in a society, which are formulated and enforced by a state organisation to regulate the relations between citizens and between the citizens and the state.   The raw material for laws are customs; marriage customs, for example, harden into laws laid down by the state and provide sanctions or penalties in the case of breach.

2. Social institutions.   The central "special" social science is concerned with social institutions, especially with those relationships within a society which are regulated by the community in general, so that a breach of them produces social disapproval.   Such regulated social relationships may be regulated by the community in general, *e.g.* marriage, or by bodies powerful enough to enforce such regulations, *e.g.* the Roman Catholic Church.

(*a*) To many sociologists sociology is the study of such social institutions, and the special social sciences such as economics and politics assist them to come to some conclusions about, for example, the family in relation to the economic or political background, or the mobility between classes as affected by the educational structure provided by the state.

(*b*) A wider view of sociology is that it is not merely a special social science providing a morphology or classification of forms of social relationships, but that it seeks to synthesise or collect together the results of the special social sciences, not merely relating these results to an institution like the family, but giving a view of the society as a whole. For example, Communism in the U.S.S.R. may be regarded as having its economic basis in the rule by an élite of party members over the masses; the élite maintains the ideology and the political control of the U.S.S.R. because its position depends on such maintenance and would be lost if a bourgeois way of life were allowed to creep in—hence the invasion of Czechoslovakia in 1968.   However, political, ethical, even religious, factors have to be taken into account and evaluated when trying to describe and explain Soviet society (*see also* XIV, **10** (*d*) (*ii*)).

3. Sociology as a specialism or a philosophy. The conception of a "general" sociology as distinct from a specialism like the other social sciences has been held by Durkheim and Hobhouse (*see* III, **12** and **18**).

(*a*) It is arguable that sociology is a *specialism* since, like the other social sciences, it seeks to correlate facts in order to arrive at conclusions concerning social relationships, which are not the whole of human life, and it uses its own methods (*see* VI).

(*b*) It cannot fail to be concerned with *values*.

(*i*) It seeks to ascertain the truth or otherwise of the *assumptions* made in the social sciences, *e.g.* that government is an evil, though a necessary one, and it examines the validity of the methods used in studying them.

(*ii*) It provides an *epistemology* of the social sciences, *i.e.* a theory of the grounds of ascertained knowledge.

(*iii*) It therefore must try to "see things whole," in Plato's phrase, to observe social facts and estimate their *significance* in relation not merely to social relationships but to human life as a whole.

SOCIAL PHILOSOPHY

4. Philosophy. The conception examined in **3** above regards sociology as being, in effect, a social philosophy.

(*a*) Philosophy is a Greek word, meaning a *love of wisdom*, or *knowledge*. (It is believed that Pythagoras was the first to use the term.) To the ancient Greeks philosophy covered the whole range of human knowledge.

(*b*) The terms *natural philosophy* and *moral philosophy* have been held to distinguish between the field of the natural sciences—mathematics, physics, etc.—and that of the sciences relating to human thought and values—logic, psychology, ethics, etc.

(*c*) Modern philosophers are not agreed upon the *definition* and *boundaries* of their study; it is sufficient for our purposes to regard philosophy as the study of the search for a true picture of the universe and man's place in it.

(*d*) *Social philosophy* will then be that field of study which seeks to determine the relation of the sciences in general to the life of society—a somewhat vague, not to say formidable, undertaking in which excessive cerebration may lead the philosopher into speculations confusing to the ordinary man, who may sympathise with the attitude of Shaw's St Joan and regard as very great nonsense what appears to the philosopher to be very great learning.

5. The aim of social philosophy. If sociology is to be more than either a broad survey of morals or customs on the one hand or a collection of detailed studies of groups or areas on the other, it must have a philosophy which can offer some guidance to values in what is called *civilisation*. For example, in February 1969, a group of scientists formed the British Society for Social Responsibility in Science with the aim of observing the activities of research scientists who carry on research without regard to the social consequences of their acts, and of setting out guidelines for future research, especially in those fields which could have the most significant consequences for society, *e.g.* nuclear research, germ weapons and genetics control. The creation of the basic elements of life in a test-tube at Cambridge in 1969 opened up possibilities which are disturbing to scientists in their capacity as citizens. The social philosophy must have the following features:

(a) It must be concerned with *ends*, whilst sociology is involved with *means*.

(b) The ends must be under *social control* if the study of means is to have any meaning; it must determine whether, for example, class mobility is an end in itself and, if so, what means could be devised for encouraging it.

(c) Social philosophy must be concerned with *values*, and it is here that even the sociologist is hampered by his own limitations (*see* I, **8** (b), and I, **10**). One may ask, with Bacon and Pontius Pilate, "What is Truth?" and ask in vain. Yet there are issues, *e.g.* the problem mentioned at the beginning of this section, on which some stand must be taken.

HISTORY AND BIOLOGY

6. History and sociology. Though history is not regarded as a special social science, the relationship between sociology and history is obviously close, for *history* is the study of the *development of people in societies.*

(*a*) To suggest that sociology deals only with the social element in history is as reasonable as the converse statement that history deals only with the historical element in the life of societies.

(*b*) Troeltsch and the German writers have sought to show that there is a fundamental difference between history and sociology, based upon the differences in the kind of knowledge they seek to attain.

(*i*) Their view emphasises the idea of the *intuitive representation of wholes* (*see* (*d*) below), an idea conceived of by the historian.

(*ii*) They regard sociology as concerned only with *social relationships,* as expressed in institutions and cultures.

(*c*) The French writers, *e.g.* Sée and Mantoux, have seen a *closer connection* between history and sociology.

(*i*) The historian is concerned with the interpretation of *concrete, specific occurrences.*

(*ii*) The sociologist is concerned with the *general laws or tendencies* of social life.

(*d*) The strictly historical interpretation of events is to regard them as *parts* of a *whole which must be interpreted intuitively e.g.* the relationship between Puritanism and capitalism is part of a whole society (see R. H. Tawney, *Religion and the Rise of Capitalism* (Murray, 1948, Penguin Books, 1966)).

(*e*) Like sociology, history has to *rely on the findings of other social sciences* like ethics and psychology.

(*f*) Neither the historian nor the sociologist can exclude references to *values.*

(*g*) When a study is concerned with *social facts, e.g.* the history of the family and its place in society, the study is sociological rather than historical. History has provided the facts; sociology interprets them in the light of other data obtained from the conclusions of other social sciences.

The study of history is now freeing itself from the old academic, not to say pedantic, concepts of the personal lives of monarchs and outstanding figures, often picturesque rather than significant. In modern times history is more concerned with *peoples* and *tendencies in social life generally,* far more, for example, with the social significance of the Nazi movement in Germany than with the acts and pronouncements of some half-mad and nearly-forgotten general, although it gives due weight to the significance of his half-madness.   It approaches, in fact, a *historical sociology*.

7. Biology and sociology.   Since human beings are a form of life, it may be suggested, as R. R. Marett did, that social anthropology, the natural history of man, is a subdivision of biology.

(*a*) However, *sociality*, the quality of being social (*see* I, **6**) as distinct from mere gregariousness, is found only in man, and it is too great a stretch of the field of biology, with its already specialised and precise disciplines, to include in it the study of human institutions.

(*b*) There have been various attempts to use *biological analogies* in sociology (*see* III, **10**), but they remain analogies, and the idea of "organs" (*e.g.* Parliament, the executive, the judiciary in a political system) cannot claim support from biological science.

(*c*) Alternatively, such discussions in the field of biology as Lamarck's theory of the inheritance of acquired characteristics and the Darwinian theories of evolution and natural selection have had a great influence on the moral and religious ideas and attitudes of Western peoples, and work on *heredity* and *environment* has contributed and must contribute a great deal to the understanding of social phenomena.   One can say, in fact, that, in view of his physical weakness and apparent tendencies to destructiveness, man has survived only because he is a social being. It may well be that investigation along the lines of relating the continued survival and progress of man to his sociality and the sociological implications of his greater control over his biological environment and life itself (*see* **5** above) will doubtless be of inestimable value.

(*d*) Whatever may be the truth of the *spiritual* nature of man, there is no doubt that *biologically* he is akin to the other primates (though not, of course, descended from apes). Desmond Morris in *The Naked Ape: A Zoologist's Study of the Human Animal* (Jonathan Cape, 1967) has thrown much light on the biological aspects of human beings, and he has shown doubts as to whether studies of "primitive" peoples are as valuable as has been supposed—social anthropology may well be dealing with offshoots and failures rather than indicating origins of social facts.

It would be fair to mention a book less entertaining and requiring a little more concentration, *Naked Ape or Homo Sapiens—A Reply to Desmond Morris*, by John Lewis and Bernard Towers (Garnstone Press, 1969). It would be profitable, too, to consider these books in conjunction with Rostow's book on the stages of economic growth (*see* **IV, 10**).

PROGRESS TEST 5

1. What are the "special" social sciences? **(1)**

2. What is meant by saying that a social institution is a "regulated social relationship"? **(2)**

3. Is sociology the study of social institutions, or does it aim to achieve a synthesis of the facts of social life? **(2)**

4. Is sociology a "specialism" like economics and law, or is there a "general" sociology? **(3)**

5. What is the nature of social philosophy? **(4)**

6. What is, or should be, the aim of social philosophy? **(5)**

7. What do you regard as the relationship between history and sociology? **(6)**

8. Is there any justification for including human institutions within the broad field of biology? **(7)**

9. What could be the possible lines of relationship between sociology and biological study? **(7)**

10. Is the idea of "organs" of society of any value to sociology? **(7)**

CHAPTER VI

THE METHODS OF SOCIOLOGY

THE NEED FOR SOCIAL SURVEYS

1. Applied sociology. If sociology, like psychology, is to have any significance in the actual life of societies, it must be applied sociology—there is no such thing as sociology for sociology's sake as there is art for art's sake. Sociology should not be the plaything of intellect, but should be a study the results of which can help the people of communities to understand themselves and their society and so take measures to free its affairs as much as possible from the doubts, uncertainties, conflicts and disturbances which trouble the life of the society and the lives of its people.

2. The scope of applied sociology. To yield results of immediate value to a society, attempts at all-embracing vistas may be left to the Platos, the Comtes and Spencers and H. G. Wellsian writers with a touch of genius and immense love for society and humankind; and efforts to understand the forces at work in a given society and a given situation should comprise the first rule of sociological method. The study of teenagers in general and over the whole world may yield some generalised results, and world-wide movements and trends may be detected, but it is of more immediate, practical—and ultimate—value to discover something about the influences that make teenagers act in a given set of circumstances, *now*. It should not then be difficult to evaluate, for example, the vested interests which induce affluent teenagers to spend their money as they do, and with courage and a sense of high purpose governments could take steps to bring such exploitation to an end. This step would not be the duty of the sociologist, nor is it within his power: all he can do is to state the facts, then the conclusions, then advise.

3. "Middle-range" sociology. The most productive approach, which has been practised for the past quarter of a century, has been the investigation of social facts based upon what Merton called "middle-range" theories (*see* **IV, 14**). There is, indeed, a *vast range of social problems* requiring examination, problems which are connected with current conditions and which may indicate the malfunctioning of society, resulting from the failure to meet the challenge of those conditions, *e.g.* juvenile delinquency, adolescence, illiteracy, drug addiction, venereal disease.

THE BASIC METHODS OF SOCIOLOGICAL ENQUIRY

4. Techniques of investigation. Techniques have been developed in the sociological investigation of "middle-range" questions, problems related to specific groups and areas, and of more narrow localised studies. In many ways they do not differ markedly from the methods employed in other fields, such as market research and business and political enquiries. Their aim is primarily to elicit information, the interpretation and evaluation of which is the business of the sociologist, who will call to his aid all that his colleagues in the special social sciences can give him. The "value judgment" on the sociologist's findings, in relation to the life of the nation as a whole, will be made by the social philosopher, or the sociologist acting as a social philosopher.

5. Questionnaires. One of the most direct and simple methods of gaining information about the experiences or attitudes of people, or a selected group of people, in relation to a given situation, is by asking them questions, either directly and personally, or by post.

(*a*) The investigator must know *precisely* what it is he wants to find out, say, about specific ways in which teenagers do or do not spend their leisure. It is not much use to ask them "what they do with themselves" in their spare time.

(*b*) The questions *should not be ambiguous:* they should be easily understood by the interviewee, and they should be capable of eliciting a precise answer. For example, "Do you go to the cinema (*i*) often, (*ii*) occasionally?" leaves varied interpretation as to the meaning of the words "often" and "occasionally."

(c) It is essential to try to *avoid bias*, even in asking the question. It is more advisable to ask "Do you avoid films with an X certificate?" than "Do you avoid torrid films?" The use of the word "torrid" would suggest that the questioner has a certain attitude towards X-certificate films.

(d) Questions relating to broad matters of conscience must be avoided where the answers will inevitably be accompanied by *qualifications*. "Do you approve of capital punishment?" is fundamentally too broad a question to be answered with a categorical "yes" or "no," except without taking much thought. Supplementary questions will have to be asked to allow for these qualifications.

(e) Many people do not bother to answer written questionnaires, especially when they are long and detailed, with various subsections, and if the questionnaires are not *taken seriously*—as seriously as they appear to be in the United States—they may offer more scope to an interviewee's sense of humour than to his desire to give an honest statement.

(f) In the interviewing of "primitive" or "simple" peoples, the investigator has to guard against *mis-statements*, *misapprehensions* and sometimes *deliberate* (if unsophisticated or childish) *attempts to mislead*.

6. Documentary material. A considerable source of information is documentary material, in forms ranging from personal letters and written statements to government publications and statistics. Radio and television documentaries are also useful, although one is apt to get five minutes' information for half an hour or so of listening.

7. The observation of social situations. The investigator may himself be able to participate in social situations, at least to the extent that he is an observer; *e.g.* he may be able to "sit in" at a management discussion on a problem, say, of a threatened strike.

8. Statistical and sampling techniques. These require a certain mathematical and technical ability in handling figures.

(a) *Sampling methods* have the advantage that results can be obtained and analysed relatively quickly; the costs are less than they would be in full-scale operations; errors can be assessed readily, and incomplete and inaccurate returns can be checked.

(b) In *random sampling* a method of selection is used which gives, as far as possible, an equal chance to all the units chosen for examination; in *stratified sampling* a sample is taken from each of the groups concerned, *e.g.* the "middle class," or the "working class"; in *multi-stage sampling*, sampling units are divided into sub-units, *e.g.* population groups may be divided into adults and non-adults; in *quota sampling*, the quotas indicate the number of people to be investigated, already divided into the types required; in *area sampling* the country is divided into grids, and parts of the grid are allocated for investigation.

(c) *Sampling errors* occur, arising from the size of the sample, from bias, and from failure on the part of the investigator to cover the whole sample—a frequent occurrence with answers to postal questionnaires.

9. Analysis of results. In analysing results obtained by statistical and sampling methods, sociologists are constantly faced with the problem of using all their pieces of evidence to provide a measure or standard for the subject concerned. In intelligence testing, the various kinds of intelligence tests such as words or numbers tests are brought together to establish a "general intelligence" factor which can be used as a measure or standard of intelligence. However, the nature of "intelligence" still merits considerable discussion.

SOCIAL SURVEYS AND SPECIAL STUDIES

10. Surveys. Social surveys are fact-finding operations in a given field.

(a) An example of a recent survey is that conducted on working-class Conservatives in urban England by Robert McKenzie and Allan Silver (see *Angels in Marble* (Heinemann, 1968)).

(i) The authors list various sources of financial support, but they found it necessary to contribute just under half of the total cost of the research themselves. The *expensive nature* of such a project is illustrated.

(*ii*) An appendix to the book describes the *sampling methods* followed in the survey.

(*b*) Margaret Stacey has written *Tradition and Change: A Study of Banbury* (Oxford University Press, 1960), the outcome of three years' field-work and six years spent in analysing and sifting the data. She writes: "The purpose of the research was to study the social structure and culture of Banbury with special reference to the introduction of large-scale industry."

(*c*) The work of Sir James Kay-Shuttleworth, Edwin Chadwick, Charles Booth and B. Seebohm Rowntree has been mentioned (*see* IV, **3** (*b*)).

(*d*) The *Social Survey Department* has been formed to ascertain facts for other government departments.

(*e*) The *Social Science Research Council* has recently been established in Britain, and the foundation may help to meet the cost of surveys, which is usually very high (*see also* XVI, **3**).

(*f*) Today the British Government publishes a great amount of *statistical information* of use to the sociologist, *e.g.* the National Census, *National Income and Expenditure, Annual Abstract of Statistics* (H.M.S.O.) and such special surveys as the Census of Distribution and the investigations which result in the production of a Retail Prices Index.

11. Producing a survey. The steps in the production of a survey are as follows:

(*a*) The precise determination of the *nature* of the problem to be investigated.

(*b*) The definition of the nature and amount of the *data* to be obtained.

(*c*) The determination of the nature of the *methods* to be employed in obtaining the desired information, *e.g.* the form of the random sample.

(*d*) The preparation of the *material* to be used in the survey, *e.g.* the designing of a questionnaire form.

(*e*) The testing of the scheme by a *pilot survey*.

(*f*) The preparation and launching of the major *field-work*.

(*g*) The *checking* of the information received for errors and inconsistencies; *e.g.* in the comparison of the information in

Dr Kinsey's famous report on the sexual behaviour of American women it was found that the sample used was over-weighted towards the young, married, ex-college woman.

(h) The *assembling* and if necessary the *tabulation* of the information received.

(i) The *classification* of the information received, *e.g.* by group or social status, which should be determined in advance.

(j) The making of the report on the survey, *adequate consultation* being made with the people concerned.

12. Case studies. These are really studies in detail of individuals or special classes of individuals, *e.g.* alcoholics, or even of groups; *e.g.* the "case studies" of management deal with more narrow problems of immediate and practical interest to the firm concerned. In a wider context, the term may be applied to studies varying in scope from Thomas and Znaniecki's *The Polish Peasant in Europe and America* (Knopf, 1927) to Young's and Willmott's *Family and Kinship in East London* (Routledge and Kegan Paul, 1957) (*see* I, **10** (c) (i)). The term, however, has no authoritative definition.

13. The comparative method. The comparative method is not so much a technique of social investigation as a way of conducting a survey by making comparisons with different areas or with groups of differing customs and ways of life and thought. The method of making comparisons is sometimes dignified by the use of such expressions as "the establishment of concomitant variations" or "cross-cultural research," distinctions being made between the sources of the data or "context," not the method of analysis.

Durkheim, in his researches on suicide (*see* I, **2**, (b) and III, 12), established an association between religious affiliation and suicide rates, showing that in predominantly Protestant countries suicide rate were three times as high as in predominantly Catholic countries. Doubtful as to whether the result could be attributed to social, cultural differences rather than to religion, he compared Protestant and Catholic provinces in Bavaria and Prussia, and obtained the same result, thereby concluding that there was a causal relationship between suicide and religious affiliation.

MEASUREMENT IN SOCIOLOGY

14. Measurement. It has been said that "science is measurement." *Sociometry*, associated with the name of J. L. Mereno, has been devised as a method of analysing and representing "attractions" and "rejections" within a given group.

(a) Sociology cannot be likened to the natural sciences, where mathematical measurement is essential. There are limits to what sociology can do in the way of measurement.

(b) Even (or especially) statistics must be treated with caution. There is the story of the sociologist who found a positive and significant correlation between the arrival of migrating storks and the periodic fluctuations in the birth rate. (*See* XI, 7, (d), NOTE.)

(c) To venture "measurement" based on vague generalisations can invite only ridicule. An article in the *Motor Market News* in 1972 suggested that a man measures his sexual potency by the size, quality and age of the car he drives. British Leyland commented: "It can't really be a general rule: if it is, all these people with minis must be hiding terrible problems." The spokesman added, with a potent realism: "It seems more likely that more money is about to buy larger cars."

15. The importance of exact definition. Definition is often more important than measurement. Barbara Wootton, who spent six years in examining social pathology with special reference to crime (see *Social Science and Social Pathology* (Allen and Unwin, 1959)), has pointed to the casualness which has characterised the definition of such an outstanding category as "the family." She pointed out that the characteristics of "broken homes" vary from one piece of research to another, and that the evidence relating to the significance of an early start in criminal behaviour is conflicting and contradictory.

It is in social demography, relating to population statistics and calculation of birth and death rates, etc., that there has been most acceptance of precise definitions and measures, *e.g.* in the ascertainment of a net reproduction rate.

PROGRESS TEST 6

1. What is "applied sociology"? **(1)**

2. What should be the scope of applied sociology? **(2)**

3. What has been the most productive approach to the study of sociological problems? **(3)**

4. What is the aim of the investigating techniques employed by the sociologist? **(4)**

5. What matters should be borne in mind when employing the questionnaire method of eliciting information? **(5)**

6. What kinds of documentary material are available? **(6)**

7. How may the investigator himself take part in a social situation? **(7)**

8. What are the advantages of sampling methods? **(8)**

9. State the variety of sampling techniques which can be employed. **(8)**

10. How do sampling errors arise? **(8)**

11. What is a major difficulty in the analysis of statistical results? **(9)**

12. (a) What is a survey? (b) Give examples of surveys which have been carried out recently. (c) What official sources of information are available? **(10)**

13. What are the steps to be taken in producing a survey? **(11)**

14. What are "case studies" in sociology? **(12)**

15. Describe the use of the comparative method. **(13)**

16. What are the difficulties of precise measurement in sociology? **(14)**

17. Why is it so important to define terms precisely in sociology? **(15)**

PART TWO

SOCIAL STRUCTURE

CHAPTER VII

THE MAIN SOCIOLOGICAL TERMS

THE MEANING OF THE SOCIOLOGICAL TERMS

1. The importance of a terminology. It has been demonstrated that in science the use of precise and universally accepted terminology is of the utmost importance, and that sociology cannot be exempted from this requirement. Agreed definitions are of particular importance in the social sciences, since so many words are used in common speech which have a special meaning in social science, as will be seen in the sections that follow. The word "society" itself, which has received considerable attention in I, **5,** is used commonly of what is described in **6** below as an "association," and similarly with the term "institution," which is defined in V, **2.**

2. The community. The basic conception in sociology is that of the community, which has been defined in I, **3** as a group of people living a common life, observing common customs and a code of general behaviour, with a background of common tradition, subject to a rule or structure of government which is accepted by all (the relation of this term to "the nation" has been discussed in I, **4**).

(a) To a great extent, the "community" is an "*ideal*" conception: it is a useful sociological generalisation, but in practice there is no continuous consciousness of belonging to the community (*see* I, **3** (*b*)).

(b) Certainly there is no such thing as a "group mind" (*see* II, **14** (*a*) and (*b*)). Only where there is an appeal to fundamental instincts and emotions, where there is a lowest common denominator, as in football hooligans and political mobs, which seeks expression in crude action, is there anything like a "common consciousness" or a "sense of belonging," and such crude action can then be adopted under the cloak of anonymity for the individual. This is a state very different from that of the concert or opera audience, in which the appreciation of the work or music depends upon the individual listener's attainments or capacity.

(c) Nevertheless, a community is a very real thing; in times of crisis or common need, the individual member thinks of the affairs of the community as a whole, even though his own personal life is at the centre of his thoughts.

3. Institutions. The meaning of social institutions has been discussed in V, 2. MacIver defined institutions as "established and recognised forms of relationships between social beings"; and Ginsberg defined them as "definite and sanctioned forms or modes of relationship between social beings in respect to one another or to some external object." The use of the term "sanctioned" must be noted: if the institution is established by the community, e.g. marriage, sanctions or penalties are imposed by the community, acting by means of a state organisation, on anyone who breaks the rules, whilst if the institution is established by another body, e.g. the celibacy of priests in the Roman Catholic Church, the body may impose the sanctions within its power.

4. Customs. The idea of sanctions is also present in customs. A custom is a traditional practice in a community; it is defined by Wundt as "a form of voluntary action that has developed in a national or tribal community." MacIver regarded customs as being the raw material of institutions; and Ginsberg, in defining custom as "sanctioned usage," is pointing to the force of general moral approval or disapproval of a particular usage. Monogamy was a custom before it became an institution; in Western societies it hardened into an institution sanctioned by the law. Social disapproval of non-observance of a custom may vary from mild censure to social isolation. Some customs, like marriage customs, may merely reflect phases in the progress of society from magical practices to the observance of customary actions expressive generally of goodwill, e.g. throwing confetti over a newly married couple, while some customs, such as raising one's hat to a lady (and often a man), or helping a lady into or out of a vehicle, are expressive of a desire to appear civilised. Some are peculiar to a group or a class (see also 11).

5. Traditions, ceremonies, rites and rituals. These terms refer to acts or observances which are not subject to such stringent sanctions as are institutions and customs, but to ways of behaviour observed for their own sake or which represent some belief or value held in common by the people who practise them.

(a) *Traditions* are general modes of thought or action which express an ideal or an honoured code; they are transmitted from generation to generation.   Some belong to the nation as a whole; *e.g.* it is the tradition in Britain to give political asylum to refugees.   Some traditions may be particular to a group or even a family; *e.g.* it may be the tradition in a particular family that the eldest son should join the Life Guards.

(b) *Ceremonies* are formal modes of behaviour publicly performed to recognise the spiritual significance of a particular act, *e.g.* the ceremony of marriage.

(c) *Rites* are used in the same way, with the difference that there is a certain solemnity attached to the occasion, *e.g.* the rite of burial or cremation.

(d) *Rituals* are routine acts attached to the performance of ceremonies and rites.   Church rituals are actions consciously performed as part of individual or group acts of worship.   Individual ritualistic or self-patterned acts are of a different category.   Sometimes they have lost all significance to the performer, and are merely habits. Frequent hand-washing may be a ritual, an act which may be of significance to the psychologist, while remaining merely a compulsive habit to the performer.

6. Associations.   Of considerable interest to the student of social structure are the associations within the community: the structure of associations is, in fact, the social structure. Within the community are smaller groups formed for the collective pursuit of some end, common to the members of the group.   They vary from small, local groups pursuing some end such as the organisation of facilities for playing tennis or learning to fly, to the wide, elaborately organised groups such as political parties, trade unions, large-scale businesses and educational and religious bodies.

(a) The characteristic of an association is that the

members share a *common interest* and are formed into a group organised to pursue that interest in common.

(*b*) Some of these interests are *pursued for their own sake*, *e.g.* the enjoyment of music; others are pursued for *interests beyond themselves, e.g.* a ratepayers' association formed for the purpose of keeping the rates low; only the accountant or the student of local government is interested in rates as a subject of professional or intellectual interest.

(*c*) A person may be a *member of a number of associations* at the same time; *e.g.* a man may be a member of a particular political party, of a church and of a tennis club, etc.

(*d*) The *relationships* between people in associations and between the associations themselves and the rest of the community, and between individuals and other individuals and groups, constitute *society* (*see also* I, **5**).

7. The special uses of terms in sociology. The expressions "society," "institution" and "association" are often used indiscriminately in ordinary language for what the sociologist would describe as an "association"; *e.g.* the Society of Authors, Playwrights and Composers, the Sherlock Holmes Society, the Institution of Mechanical Engineers and the Institution of Civil Engineers are all associations.

8. The institutionalising of associations. Some associations are so all-embracing in their scope and power that they have become institutionalised, *i.e.* they are regarded as institutions in themselves; sometimes the collected associations in the community are together conceived of as an institution.

(*a*) The fundamental association in society is the *family association*; everyone must belong at birth to a family association of mother and child (unless test-tube babies take over the present organization of society) and the family association is the normal and common association of parents and children. The family association in general has been so much subject to customary and legal sanctions that "the family" or "the Family" is used as a collective noun connoting these relationships and sanctions in the sense of an institution.

(*b*) Similarly, the *state*, the association embracing everybody in the community and consisting of the governed and the government, is conceived of as an institution.   The nature of the state, its purposes and powers, and the role which it should play in the life of society, have been discussed by philosophers from Plato onwards (*see* II).

(*i*) The sanctions of the state are legal.   *Laws* are rules formulated and approved by the community (as represented by the *legislature* of the state) to regulate the relations between individuals as citizens and between citizens and the government.

(*ii*) The laws are carried out by the *executive* of the state (in Britain "the Crown") and their interpretation is in the hands of the *judiciary*, the decisions of the judiciary being enforced by the organisation of the police and the legal system.

(*c*) The *Church*, in medieval days, in the time of "Christendom" and the "Holy Roman Empire," was the Roman Catholic Church, the universal Church to which all Christians belonged.   The established Church in England is now the Anglican Church.

(*i*) The "Church" is now used as an expression to describe the various religious associations of the nation as a whole or to denote the Christian organisations in general.

(*ii*) A church is a particular religious body.

(*iii*) As an institution, the Church, when it is not specifically the Roman Catholic Church (or any similar body like the Greek Orthodox Church), is that organisation of religious life the sanctions of which apply to its members.   The expression needs careful handling by the sociologist.

THE STRUCTURE OF A SOCIETY

9. The complexity of the social structure.   It should now be clear what is meant by the expression "social structure"— it is the structure of institutions and associations within a community.

(*a*) These institutions and associations are generally so complex in a modern, industrialised community that it is often more fruitful to discuss the structure of groups or types of organisations, *e.g.* trade unions or political parties, and try to assess their significance in the life of the community, than to attempt to understand them all together at once.

(b) The structure of associations and institutions is by no means rigid and permanent. The social structure is *dynamic*: it is subject to modifications which either enable it to respond to changing circumstances and so retain a degree of stability, or break it down so that a new order has to be constructed, *e.g.* after the explosion of the French Revolution.

(i) The life of the city-state in ancient *Greece* blossomed into a high civilisation in the fifth century B.C., but could not withstand the stresses of internecine strife, slavery and the lack of moral standards.

(ii) *Rome* was modified from a city-state into an empire, but the empire could not withstand the stresses brought about by the overloading of its administrative and military resources, the inadequacy of technology, slavery and, again, the decay of the moral fibre in the people.

(iii) The *feudal communities* which were established after the break-up of the Roman Empire based rights on the possession of land. They were closed economies, with a policy of "no-change" in production methods, which were doomed to destruction as towns developed, merchant and craft guilds were organised, markets expanded and a national consciousness replaced local community consciousness in the conception of the "community."

(iv) The *village communities* of Europe, based on the household, showed a certain degree of stability: the Russian *mir* was abolished as late as 1861.

10. The social system in the modern nation-state. The social system in the modern nation-state is not a *system* at all, in the sense that it is a structure consciously designed by a great intelligence or a body of intelligences, in which the social, economic and political details of the system are set out with a code of rules and regulations to be imposed by the "guardians" or "philosopher-king." It is a complex which is the result of a series of changes and adaptations. Its features include the following:

(a) A high and expanding level of *industrial development* (*see* IV, **9, 10**).
(b) An increasing importance of *capital* in economic development.
(c) *Population* pressure (*see* XV).
(d) Changes in *class structure* (*see* IX).

(e) *Economic and political organisations.*
(f) *Mass communications.*
(g) The *organisation of labour.*

SOCIAL CULTURE

11. The culture of a society. The difficulties of defining and illustrating social structure apply even more forcibly to the concept of "culture." The early anthropologists interpreted the word broadly to include such subjects as law, customs, morals and beliefs.

(a) The Americans have laid an emphasis on *symbolism*: A. Kroeber and Talcott Parsons, "The Concepts of Culture and Social System" in the *American Sociological Review* (October, 1958), write of culture as "the transmitted and created patterns of values, ideas and other symbolic, meaningful systems in the shaping of human behaviour." The similar emphasis on symbolism by G. Jaeger and P. Selznick in "A Normative View of Culture" in the *American Sociological Review* (October, 1964) indicates that there is a conception of an *ideal* which seems to have been derived from Max Weber's idea of ideal types (*see* III, 11 (d)).

(b) The behaviour of people in society has been both the *cause* and the *result* of the complex of relationships of morals, customs, tradition, rites, rituals and ceremonies and of the institutions and associations which make up the structure of society. The ways in which this complex of activities and ideas manifests itself as a *way of life*, characterised by certain standards of *behaviour*, *belief* and *conduct* generally, is the *culture* of a nation, a community or a group. One can speak of a British culture, a French culture and the culture of the "middle class" or the "upper class," manifesting itself, for example, in an addiction to cricket.

(c) Once again, culture-creating is a *dynamic* process; *e.g.* changes in morals and other facets of social life have made cock-fighting and bear-baiting no longer acceptable sports in Britain.

12. Role and status. In the organisational structure of associations and in the community generally, there will be certain positions occupied by individual persons; *e.g.* a headship of a household, a directorship of an industrial company, an Under-Secretaryship in the Civil Service.

(*a*) The *status* is the position a person holds in the hierarchy of which he forms a part, as in the above examples.

(*i*) A status may be *ascribed*, or previously *determined, e.g.* the status of the youngest son in a family.

(*ii*) A status may be *achieved*, as when a man becomes a Minister in the Government by his own efforts.

(*b*) The *role* is the pattern of behaviour which is expected by the community or by a particular group of the person who occupies a given status: for example, not only does one *not expect* a clergyman to act as a comedian on television in his spare time; it is expected of him that he shall *not* do so.

(*i*) A role may be *ascribed*, as when it is expected that the eldest son of a family shall become a naval officer.

(*ii*) A role may be *achieved*, as when, for example, a person who feels temperamentally unfitted to become a teacher, yet is forced by circumstances to become one, achieves the necessary qualities enabling him to earn the respect of his pupils.

(*c*) An individual may exchange many roles or statuses throughout life. This process of change may take place in institutions like the family or the Church, or in moral or religious concerns, or with a group, as in the position of women through history, or with nations, as when the Czechoslovak people were brought back after 1968 onwards to the status of a subordinate state by the U.S.S.R.

PROGRESS TEST 7

1. Why is terminology of such importance in sociology? **(1)**

2. What is a community? Is there a "group consciousness" in a community? **(2)**

3. What are institutions? Give examples. **(3)**

4. What are customs? **(4)**

5. Define traditions, ceremonies, rites and rituals. Give examples. **(5)**

6. What are associations, as understood in sociology? Give examples. **(6)**

7. Give examples of associations often spoken of in common speech as "societies" or "institutions." (7)

8. Why are the family, the state and the Church often referred to as institutions? (8)

9. Why is the social structure "dynamic"? (9)

10. Is the social system a "system"? (10)

11. What is the "culture" of a society? (11)

12. Define (a) status, (b) role. (12)

13. Define (a) ascribed status, (b) achieved status. (12)

14. How can statuses and roles change? (12)

CHAPTER VIII

KINSHIP AND THE FAMILY

THE FAMILY AS AN ASSOCIATION

1. The family as the fundamental unit of social life. Every-body starts life in a family, even if it is only a family of two—mother and child. With the normal family of mother, father, brothers and sisters, there is established an association which from its fundamental importance in human life is often spoken of as an institution (*see* VII, **8** (*a*)). To whatever "modern-istic" regions imagination may range, the *fact* of the family is hardly likely to disappear, for belonging to a family is part of being human.

2. Status and role in the family. The relationships in which members of a family stand to one another are subject to the rules regarding status and role which society expects (*see* VII, **12**). Thus, the husband, for example, has a status and a role, and there is a conjugal role played by the husband and wife; the eldest son may have a definite status, especially when there is a question of succession to a higher status.

3. Terms used by social anthropologists. The complex relationships existing between people living in family groups in primitive societies have inspired social anthropologists to define their terms carefully. These terms have been applied to relationships in modern societies—which are not so far removed from "primitive" societies as some people imagine.

(*a*) In simple societies most statuses are *ascribed* (*see* VII, **12** (*a*) (*i*)); *i.e.* they depend upon a person's birth. Hence *kinship*, real or related to the method used for tracing relationship, is of the greatest importance.

(*b*) The *nuclear* family is the simple "legal" family, a couple with a child or children, recognised as a family from the fact that the couple are married, as distinguished from a *natural* family, a wider term used to describe a family in which the mother and father may not be married.

(c) Descent in primitive societies is traced either through the male parent, *i.e. patrilineal* descent, or through the female parent, *i.e. matrilineal* descent.

(d) A *sibling* is one of two or more children having one or both parents in common.   Where parents and siblings live together or in close proximity and regard themselves as forming one large family, the family is an *extended* family.

4. Marriage rules and sanctions.   The marriage rules of a people may demand or permit various forms; sanctions are often of great severity, since ideas on marriage and child-bearing are connected with ideas of supernatural agencies. The definition given in **3** above and the following sections are sufficient for the student of sociology who is not particularly concerned with social anthropology.

(a) *Monogamy* is the marriage of one man to one woman.

(b) *Polygamy* is a general term embracing the two following kinds of marriages:

(i) *Polygyny*, the marriage of one man to more than one woman (the term "polygamy" is often used to mean polygyny).

(ii) *Polyandry*, the marriage of one woman to more than one man.

(c) *Endogamy* comprises rules prohibiting marriage with a person who is not a member of one's group.

(d) *Exogamy* comprises the rules prohibiting marriage with a person who is a member of one's group.

5. The family in pre-industrial England.   In *The Listener*, 7th April, 1960, Peter Laslett described the composition of the household of a London baker in 1619.   The family consisted of the baker and his wife, four journeymen (those workers who had completed their apprenticeship), two apprentices, two maidservants and the baker's three children: thirteen in all. The baker was the head of the family, and there was no distinction between his domestic and economic functions.   In rural England, family life was carried on in the same way. There was no group of persons larger than a family—a group, that is, subject to sanctions similar to those of the family.

6. The family in modern industrial England. The picture of the family in a modern industrialised community is very different.

(*a*) The state has taken over more and more of the functions of the family.

(*i*) In *education*, the great majority of schools, attended by 90 per cent of schoolchildren, are maintained or assisted out of public funds, as are most technical colleges and colleges for further education: through the University Grants Committee, the central government contributes over 70 per cent of the current expenditure of universities and about 90 per cent of their capital programmes.

(*ii*) The state co-operates with local authorities in the provision of a *youth employment* service.

(*iii*) Most voluntary *youth organisations* receive grants from the central and local government authorities.

(*iv*) In all kinds of *welfare*, the services such as those providing for the health and food of schoolchildren and child protection have superseded the sometimes doubtful care exercised by the family.

(*b*) *Economic activities* are now carried on by private business concerns, sometimes of great size, and by public corporations, and the family is no longer the self-contained unit of economic organisation (*see also* XIII).

(*c*) *Moral and religious training* is no longer a simple matter of co-operation between home and Church. A daily school service and religious instruction are (at the moment of writing) provided by the schools. The teachings of the Church are assailed by various vested interests making powerful suggestions to the young, especially to the susceptible teenager with money to spend, and "permissiveness" in matters of morality has been attended by a *laissez-faire* attitude on the part of an otherwise paternalistic government.

(*d*) The greater mobility derived from modern methods of *transport and communications* may tend physically to split the family; but likewise, those means of transport and communication enable the members of the family to keep in contact with one another.

7. The break-up of the family. Such considerations have prompted writers with, perhaps, too great an attachment to

the "classical" view of the family to suggest that the family
as an institution is in the process of decay (see Bertrand
Russell, *Marriage and Morals* (Allen and Unwin, 1932)).   Carl
Zimmerman, in *Family and Civilisation* (Harper, 1947), wrote
of "the family's present trend towards a climactic break-up."
The Report of the Royal Commission on Population (1949),
in the article *Social Policy and the Family* (paras. 402–6,
pp. 149–51) noted the influence of the social services on the size
of the family.   The "consanguine" family of Victorian times,
consisting of near relatives, has been reduced to the "conjugal" family, providing the bare essentials of the home for
the upbringing of the young children and providing for the
sexual and mutual comfort for the partners.

8. Reasons for the disintegration of the family.   The change
to the "nuclear" family, consisting only of the parents and
dependent children, the "nuclear" essentials, has been attributed to such factors as occupational mobility, housing
developments and the creation of new towns.   Talcott
Parsons in *Essays in Sociological Theory, Pure and Applied*
(Free Press, 1949) attached importance to high geographical
and occupational mobility.   J. M. Mogey in *Family and
Neighbourhood* (Oxford University Press, 1956), studying the
differences between a new housing estate and an older neighbourhood centre, wrote that the housing estate encouraged
the "nuclear" family.

It is interesting to observe that the nuclear family is found
in certain "classes."   The well-known study of M. Young and
P. Willmott, *Family and Kinship in East London* (Routledge
and Kegan Paul, 1957), indicated that in the East End of
London, in Bethnal Green, the extended family existed, including within it three and even four generations.   The ties
between mother and daughter and grandchildren were particularly strong and "Mum" was the important figure in the
hierarchy.   The same authors investigated a middle-class
London suburb, Woodford, and they found that there was less
emphasis on kinship than in Bethnal Green (*Family and Class
in a London Suburb* (Routledge and Kegan Paul, 1960)).

Generally, in the larger towns, in the "dormitory" towns,
in the new towns and in the south of England, there appears
to be a greater separation from "Mum" and the extended
family than in the smaller towns, in the working-class districts,

and in the villages where a community spirit prevails. There are strong family attachments in certain localities, *e.g.* South Wales. There seems, however, to have been an undue emphasis by some sociologists on facts such as these. Some, indeed, appear to have been surprised that there is such a thing as human love at all.

In spite of all the forecasts about its imminent dissolution, the family continues to exist. The changes which have affected the family as an association and the position of its members, and changes in the marriage laws and customs, which are discussed in the following sections, have caused structural alterations which do not produce the kind of conflicts which threaten the stability of society itself (*see* IV, **17**).

RECENT CHANGES IN THE FAMILY STRUCTURE

9. The most important changes. The kinds of changes which have occurred in Britain and in the Western world generally, and which have affected the relationships within the family units and hence the family structure, relate mainly to the size of the family, the structure of households, the position of women and divorce rates.

10. The size of the family. David C. Marsh, quoting from the Report of the Royal Commission on Population, 1949, and its Papers, and from the Censuses of 1911 and 1951, has discussed in *The Changing Social Structure of England and Wales, 1871–1961* (Routledge and Kegan Paul, 1965) statistics relating to the size of the family:

(*a*) Whereas in the nineteenth century families of four or more children constituted the majority (72 per cent), in the twentieth century they are the minority (20 per cent).

(*b*) The reduction has not been uniform throughout social groups. In the latter part of the nineteenth century the decline in family size was more rapid in the professional and employing classes, and in the early years of the twentieth century the gap between the average size of family in the "upper" and "lower" social classes (these terms being based upon the occupation of the husband) became wider. After the First World War the trend towards smaller families spread to all social classes.

11. Reasons for the reduction of family size. There are a number of possible explanations, which are as follows:

(*a*) The main factor appears to have been the greater efficiency and more widespread acceptance of *contraceptive methods*, due to changes in the moral climate, making contraception at least in non-Catholic countries no longer a matter of conscience.

(*i*) Birth rates—always unpredictable—have been affected since the contraceptive "Pill" became generally available in Britain in 1961. In 1961 3,000 women were believed to be taking the "Pill." There were 811,281 births in England and Wales. Births continued to rise until they reached a peak of 875,972 in 1964, when they declined to 849,823 in 1966. The birth rate declined from 18·9 per thousand in 1963 to 18·1 per thousand in 1967.

(*ii*) During those four years the number of women known to be taking birth-control pills increased from 120,000 to nearly 800,000, although the Family Planning Association believes that the figure is nearer one million.

(*iii*) It has been estimated that the effect of the contraceptive pill has been to cut the births in Britain by 25,000 a year.

(*iv*) The effects of the pill on fertility, sex desire and the general health of women are still a matter of controversy.

(*b*) Another reason has been the changes in the *economic position* of the family in relation to the availability of consumer goods, a new car perhaps being preferred to an additional child in the family.

(*c*) The greater *freedom of women* has been a very powerful influence (*see* **12** below).

12. The position of women. In the nineteenth century, all the wife's personal chattels became, on marriage, the absolute property of her husband, who could also dispose of her leasehold property during his life and who enjoyed her freehold estate during her life. Women attained political equality with men only in the early twentieth century. With the demand for female labour during the two world wars, and the greater opportunities for entering the professions, the economic and social statuses of women changed and, accordingly, the roles of the woman as housekeeper, mistress and mother (*see* VII, **12**).

(*a*) The ability to *plan births* and *avoid pregnancy* has given women more power over their own lives and personalities.

(*b*) More married and single women go out to work, which has meant greater *economic independence* for middle- and working-class women and has provided them at least with the opportunities to employ their leisure in educative ways as well as superficially to achieve a higher status, *e.g.* a second car, holidays abroad, better clothes.

(*i*) In 1961 nearly 52 per cent of the women in Britain were gainfully employed, compared with 50 per cent in 1951.

(*ii*) Of all married women, nearly one in three was gainfully occupied in 1961, compared with one in four in 1951.

(*iii*) A survey carried out by W. G. Runciman in 1962 showed that while 40 per cent of the wives of manual workers had full- or part-time jobs, the percentage was only 30 per cent for the wives of non-manual workers.

(*c*) *Labour-saving devices* have lessened the burden of household work.

(*d*) Greater equality between the sexes now extends to the sphere of housework. Young and Willmott, in their study of families in east London (*see* **8**), found that thirty-two of the forty-five husbands in the marriage sample helped with the housework.

(*e*) The children may be better off when their mothers go out to work. Pearl Jephcott, Nancy Seear and J. H. Smith, in *Married Women Working* (Allen and Unwin, 1962), reported that in Bermondsey children of working mothers were healthier, more regular in their attendance at school, and achieved better results in the eleven-plus examinations than the children of non-working mothers.

(*f*) The *Matrimonial Proceedings and Property Act, 1970*, made it possible for a divorced wife to be given an interest in the home on account of being a housewife. In a case before the Appeal Court in February, 1973, whilst a wife's interest in the family home was reduced from a half to a third, Lord Denning, the Master of the Rolls, said Parliament recognised that the wife who looks after the home contributes as much to the home as the woman who goes out to work.

Under the *Matrimonial Homes Act*, 1967, a wife (or a

husband whose wife owns their house) can enter a charge at the Land Registry to protect their rights of occupation. The scope and operation of the Act have been criticised.

In the report of the Law Commission, 6th June 1973, the view is expressed that husbands and wives should own their houses equally.

NOTE: Such studies must always be considered in their context. The facts of social classes (discussed in the next chapter) may often restrict the validity of conclusions about a given group-culture (*see* VII, **11**).   Even a "holiday abroad" may mean a very different thing to a middle-class and a working-class tourist.

13. Marriage and divorce. The fact that a heading "marriage and divorce" arouses no idea of incongruity in the mind of the modern Westerner is significant.   The question arises as to whether people nowadays enter into marriage more light-heartedly than before, with perhaps divorce as an insurance by which the attempt at a lasting marriage can be abandoned if it does not seem to be working out success-fully.

14. Marriage statistics. In 1955 there were some 358,000 marriages in England and Wales; by 1965 there were 371,127; in 1968, 407,822.   Official statistics reveal that for England and Wales the mean age at first marriage was, between 1911 and 1915, 27·9 years for men and 25·75 for women. In 1964 the figures showed 25·24 years for men and 22·78 for women.   The general tendency is for the number of marriages to increase and for the average age to fall.   The 1972 Registrar General's report shows that during the decade 1961–70, the average age of brides dropped from 23·13 years to 22·38 years and of grooms, from 25·59 to 24·43 years.   In 1969, Shelter, the national campaign for the homeless, felt it necessary, in a booklet entitled *A Home of Your Own*, to warn *school-leavers* and other young people in overcrowded areas not to expect to get a council house when they married.

15. Divorces. From 1857, divorce could be obtained in Britain by means other than by Act of Parliament.   In 1925 limited legal aid became available to poorer people to obtain a divorce.   After 1937, there was an extension of the grounds for divorce and nullity petitions. The *Divorce Reform Act*, 1969, has altered the grounds for divorce and judicial separation: section 1 provides that in future the *sole grounds* for divorce shall be that the marriage has broken down irretrievably. A single act of adultery will not be sufficient evidence to establish a breakdown. The former grounds for judicial separation have been abolished and are now those mentioned in the Act (section 2), *i.e.* those relating to the breakdown of a marriage.

Between 1901 and 1905, the average number of petitions for divorce was 810: in 1961 it was 31,900. Statistics show that the number of marriages likely to end in divorce had risen from 0·2 per cent in 1911 to 6·7 per cent by 1964. From 1960 to 1965 the rate of failure in marriage rose by 58 per cent to 43,000 a year, and the number of divorce decrees made absolute rose from 23,000 in 1958 to over 37,000 in 1965.

Between 1961 and 1970 the rate of divorce doubled: from 2·1 per thousand marriages to 4·7. The peak of divorces, 60,000, was reached immediately after the Second World War; by the end of 1970, immediately before the new *Divorce Act* came into operation, the number of divorces reached the second highest level of 58,000.

In the U.S.A., about 2,000 divorces per day were being granted in 1970; the rate was 1,000 per day in 1960. One in three marriages was being dissolved in 1970.

(*a*) The majority of breakdowns in marriages occur among the young. In 1959, the rate for separations for women who were under twenty when they married was about four times as high as the rate for separated couples as a whole. The Registrar-General's report referred to above shows that 85 per cent of the divorced wives had married before they were 25, whilst less than 10 per cent of the divorces were of those who had married between the ages of 25 and 30.

In the U.S.A., 54 per cent of teen-age marriages end in divorce; 36 per cent end in divorce when only the bride is teen-age; and 18 per cent end in divorce when both bride and groom are twenty years of age or older.

(*b*) "Shot-gun" marriages are more likely to break down than marriages contracted where the bride was not pregnant. In 1960 one in five brides in Great Britain was pregnant. (*See also* XI, **7**.)

(c) Divorce rates are highest for childless couples, and decline as the family size increases.

NOTE: Statistics must be treated with caution: there is no need to rush to alarmist conclusions.

(i) Over 90 per cent of marriages in Britain do *not* end in divorce—a much higher percentage of successful marriages than in the U.S.A.

(ii) The increase in the divorce rate does not mean that marriage as an institution is breaking down. Seven of every hundred broken marriages in Britain are replaced by four new marriages, and more couples are remarrying. In 1961, the rate or remarriage was $16 \cdot 2$ per cent for men and $9 \cdot 2$ per cent for women; by 1970 the figures had risen to $18 \cdot 9$ per cent for men and $11 \cdot 5$ per cent for women.

16. The family and the home. It seems that the *home* has not lost its significance as the centre of life and the refuge from the stresses of the world outside, and conjugal relationships and the protection, comfort and teaching of children appear to be strengthened.

(a) Young and Willmott. in their study of families in east London (*see* **8** above) found that the husbands became more home-centred with the removal of young families to housing estates in the outer suburbs.

(b) Margaret Stacey in *Tradition and Change: A Study of Banbury* (Oxford University Press, 1960) says that the family in Banbury remained particularly important in two respects: in teaching fundamental social and moral attitudes, and in its influence upon social status. She speaks of the family as "still the giver of many of the patterns of social behaviour."

(c) It would seem that all the attention given to the subject of the family by sociologists, the concern expressed as to its welfare, and even the attacks of the *avant-garde* upon it, are evidence of the continued vigour of the family as a social institution rather than indicative of its decline and imminent decease.

PROGRESS TEST 8

1. Why is the family association "the fundamental unit of social life"? **(1)**

2. How do status and role occur in the family? **(2)**

3. Why is kinship important in primitive societies? **(3)**

4. Define (a) the "nuclear family"; (b) the "natural family"; (c) patrilineal and matrilineal descent; (d) a sibling; (e) the extended family. **(3)**

5. Define the following terms: (a) monogamy; (b) polygamy; (c) polygyny; (d) polyandry; (e) endogamy; (d) exogamy. **(4)**

6. What persons were included in the family group in pre-industrial England? **(5)**

7. What influences does the industrialisation of society bring to bear on the family? **(6)**

8. What changes have been held responsible for the alleged break-up of the structure of the family in recent years? **(8)**

9. What changes have been related to the structure of the family? **(9)**

10. What changes have occurred in family size during the twentieth century? **(10)**

11. What have been the factors responsible for this change? **(11)**

12. What factors have affected the position of women in the twentieth century? **(12)**

13. What trends do marriage statistics show? **(13, 14)**

14. What trends do the divorce statistics show? **(15)**

15. What is the significance of the "home" in the family association? **(16)**

CHAPTER IX

SOCIAL CLASSES

THE MEANING OF SOCIAL CLASS

1. The family environment. The immediate social environment of the family comprises the social class or group to which the family belongs. In medieval days the family was the centre of education and of religious and moral life, and its social status was determined by the economic and political hierarchy of the feudal system. The factors which have been observed in VIII, **6,** the effects of industrialisation, have been active in the determination of social classes.

2. Social divisions in the nineteenth century. In the nineteenth century social classes were clearly defined according to income and occupation. In *Sybil, or The Two Nations*, written by Disraeli, and published in 1845, Egremont says: "I was told that an impassable gulf divided the Rich from the Poor; I was told that the Privileged and the People formed Two Nations, governed by different laws, influenced by different manners, with no thoughts or sympathies in common; with an innate inability of mutual comprehension." Contrasting the mental states of, say, hysterical "pop music" audiences and audiences at one of the lesser-known operas in this country, it is possible to suggest that such impassable gulfs may still exist.

3. Industrialisation and social class. When England was a mainly agricultural country, classes were almost as sharply differentiated as they were under the feudal system. The aristocracy enjoyed wealth and power derived from the ownership of land, with ways of thought and an attitude of authority derived from their environment; the tenant farmers and country squires had their own tradition and culture, demonstrated by their resistance to Charles I and his pretensions in the Civil Wars of 1642 to 1649; the agricultural labourer had a status and role derived from his rights and duties on the farm and his holding. Even under the domestic system the head of the household retained certain rights and duties in relation to the land. All these classes had a stake in the land.

(a) The *fact* of social class was frankly recognised, as in the expression "the quality," used of the upper middle and aristocratic classes.

(b) The migration to the towns and the loss of the peasants' holdings meant that the new dispossessed industrial working class had no stake in the land, *no sense of responsibility* to the community in general.

(c) Industrialisation and the increase in population, the division of labour, the formation of trade unions and the increasing antagonism between management and unionists and between unionists themselves, affected by the memories of the years of depression between the wars, have helped to change the class structure from one of *acceptance* of the social order to a *struggle* for dominance, the latest phase of which occurred in 1971, when the workers at the Upper Clyde Shipyards staged a "work-in," refusing to accept redundancies and closure of the yards. It was in effect a refusal to accept unemployment. The subsequent "confrontation" between the Government and the trade unions on the issues of the *Industrial Relations Act*, 1971, and a prices and incomes policy, have been nothing as dramatic as the "class war" foretold by Karl Marx (*see* II, **18** (*g*) and III, **15**) but rather an irritation at the effects on the affluence referred to in (*d*) below of rising prices accentuated by decimalisation of the currency and the pains of entering into the European Economic Community. It is dangerous to pass judgment on the significance of current events; but a desire for higher wages, shorter hours and longer holidays, common to all people engaged in dull labour rather than creative work, accompanied by an understandable reluctance to delve into the intricacies of economic theory, and accompanied also by a resentment at inequalities of income, need not necessarily be construed as "the first shots in the class war."

(d) In the "affluent society," with its high wages and defiance of management discipline, the "working classes" have sought to *emulate* the conditions of living of the middle classes, expressed mainly in the possession of material goods such as motor-cars and in taking holidays abroad.

(*e*) There has arisen a *new class* consisting of lower-grade civil servants, local government officers, insurance and bank employees, etc.; it includes also a professional class of higher clerical and lower managerial grades, seeking professional status in the formation of professional associations. In 1801, this kind of worker constituted 2 per cent of the employed population; by 1951 this group comprised 5 per cent—about two million people (see R. Lewis and A. Maude, *The English Middle Classes* (Penguin Books, 1953)).

4. The definition of "class."   With the disappearance of the old well-defined hierarchy, and the development of conditions observed in **3**, it has become exceedingly difficult to define what is meant by "social class."   There are people who will deny altogether that social classes exist today, contending that in Britain the "classless society"—meaning by that the "one-class" society—has been attained.   Nevertheless, social classes do exist.

(*a*) In general, people of the same social class *mingle together*, adopt the same modes of speech and habits of conduct, enjoy the same kind of entertainment and have the same tastes in the arts and music.

(*b*) The above is, of course, very general, and may have little reference to wealth or occupation.   Perhaps at least for one class, the middle class, a male member of which may aspire to that somewhat loosely-defined description, a "gentleman," there is a *code of conduct* similar to that acquired by the best public-school training, a quiet confidence, a courtesy resembling that attributed to worthy knights of the Middle Ages.   It is in modern times a conduct which would be regarded as "civilised."   The "affluent society," however, has brought with it not merely an expected congestion of the roads by cars, but a conduct which is unbecoming to "civilised" behaviour: it is not "civilised," for example, to carry on one's rear window such threats or warnings as "If you can read this you are too damned close" or "If I stop—can you?"

(*c*) The frequent use of quotation marks in discussions about class structure (a general phenomenon in sociology where a jargon has not been invented to cover up ignorance) indicates that there is a *vagueness* about classes which is not solved by the ability to pin-point such sub-groups as "the county class" or "the hunting class" or the class which drops fish-and-chip papers, orange peel and cigarette packets in the street.   One reason for this is that it is no longer of such significance to adopt such a standard classification as "manual" and "non-manual" classes, "professional" and "non-professional," and so on; educational opportunities, the redistribution of incomes and the opportunities to display qualities of character and ability have been responsible for blurring the lines of distinction between the classes.

DETERMINING SOCIAL CLASS

5. The determinants of social class. One must, however, attempt some method of classification or, at least, a description of the classes.   The meaning of the "aristocratic" or "upper" class is clear enough; the members of this class constitute about 2 per cent of the population in Britain. Below this are the "middle" and "working" classes who form a very mixed conglomeration—the term "working class" itself is now very nearly out of date.

It is not much help to quote the occupational distribution of the population as given in such publications as the *Gazette* of the Department of Employment (formerly the Ministry of Labour).   The determinants of social class today, many and various as they are, may be classified broadly as follows:

    (a) Income, occupation and profession.
    (b) Education.
    (c) Subjective assessments.
    (d) Family environment and general behaviour.
    (e) Leisure activities, including political behaviour.

6. Income, occupation and profession. Occupation has been, and to some extent still is, the most popular criterion of social class.   Though incomes of manual workers and of manual-worker households where more than one member of the family goes out to work may be higher than those of some professional workers, the ultimate stability, security and traditional pride in the family occupation may well be lacking.

This pride is a "professionalism" based on education and training and professional skill and the consciousness of belonging to a class of professional probity, *e.g.* medicine, the law. It cannot be attained by, *e.g.*, pop-singers, even though they may acquire huge incomes, but it is possessed by, *e.g.*, opera singers. This factor is probably of greater importance than the more concrete considerations resulting in the sixteen "socio-economic" groups identified in the 1961 Census (see David C. Marsh, *The Changing Social Structure of England and Wales 1871–1961* (Routledge and Kegan Paul, 1965)). Market research organisations base their assessments on income and occupation but the inadequacy of such classifications is that, though they define income and occupation groups, social class in modern times means much more than mere identification with such groups, and the classifications take no account of *psychological considerations.*

NOTE: The Monopolies Commission, in its 1970 report, made tentative references to restrictive practices in the *professions*, but the report passed no judgment on particular practices.

7. Education. The *Education Act* of 1902, providing secondary education for everybody, and the 1944 *Education Act*, replacing the classification of publicly aided education in England and Wales into primary and secondary education by a new classification into primary, secondary and further education, brought to a logical conclusion the process begun by the 1870 Act which provided popular elementary education. There has been considerable progress in the attitude of the governmental authorities who, in 1820, set up a Select Committee on the Education of the Lower Orders.

(*a*) These Acts, together with the provisions made for the development of further education in technical colleges and the opportunities for *technological* and *university* education, have transformed the educational background of the mass of the population.

(*b*) Surveys confirm that a considerable portion of the population believe that a *connection* exists between social class and the educational background of a person. Indeed, the phrase "the public-school class" is accepted as a sufficient description of those people who went to public schools.

(c) The total school population of the United Kingdom rose from 8·4 million in the year 1955–6 to 9·1 million in the year 1965–6. The vast majority of the pupils were in *maintained* schools (*i.e.* schools maintained by the local education authorities) and other grant-aided schools. (*See* X, **5**, NOTE.)

(d) The extension of secondary and university education in Britain has resulted in a change in the proportion of *university* students coming from the different types of schools.

(i) In the 1930s only one-third of university entrants came from the local authority and grant-aided schools; in the 1950s two-thirds came from the local authority and grant-aided schools and one-third from the independent schools (including public schools).

(ii) The Robbins Committee, which reported in 1963 on full-time higher education in Britain, calculated that 63 per cent of university undergraduates came from local education authority schools, 15 per cent from direct-grant schools (*i.e.* schools providing for a certain number of free places) and only 22 per cent from independent schools.

(e) The dilution of the secondary grammar school system by the introduction of *comprehensive schools* (in place of the old grammar school and secondary modern school) has been held by some to have been a Socialist, egalitarian movement inspired essentially by class-consciousness. Whatever its inspiration, and whatever greater opportunities for "upgrading" its pupils it may provide, it cannot, educationally, destroy the distinction between a "grammar school type" and other "types."

(f) Children of the professional classes tend to *stay at school longer* than children in the manual-worker class, and seek professional qualifications themselves.

8. Subjective assessments. There is obviously greater class mobility as the result of educational opportunities and the spread of mass communications. The difficulty of estimating the *degree* of class mobility arises largely from the fundamental difficulty associated with the definition of social class itself. Subjective assessments, *i.e.* estimates made by oneself, have the disadvantage that the concept of a particular class does not mean the same thing to all people.

(a) A British Institute of Public Opinion poll in 1952 showed that the number of people content to describe themselves as "working class" had declined considerably since an enquiry in 1946.

(b) In "Some Subjective Aspects of Social Stratification" (*Social Mobility in Britain*, Ed. D. V. Glass (Routledge and Kegan Paul, 1954), F. M. Martin stated that one quarter of "black-coated" workers described themselves as "working class" and one-quarter of manual workers described themselves as "middle class."

(c) Willmott and Young's survey of Woodford, *Family and Class in a London Suburb* (Routledge and Kegan Paul, 1960) showed that 48 per cent of the 355 manual workers in their sample described themselves as "middle class."

9. Family environment and general behaviour. There is hardly need to observe that family background and the general social environment must have a great influence on determining social class for all but the most independent and gifted minds.

(a) The *home background* and immediate environmental influences, the *ways of life* and *manners of speech* must influence both objective and subjective assessments of social class. The child who speaks "standard southern English" in the school play and reverts to the local dialect at home is adjusting his home "class" mode of speech to the demands of a particular and, in some ways, alien environment.

The report of the National Children's Bureau study published in June 1972, referred to the extent and scope of the disadvantages likely to be suffered by the "working class" child:

"Compared to his middle class contemporary, the seven-year-old working class child is 1·3 inches shorter, is more likely to squint, more likely to have a speech defect, more likely to wet his bed, and more likely to have trouble adjusting at school."

(*The Guardian*, 3 June 1972)

(b) *Trends of fashion* may influence temporarily ways of speech and conduct which indicate changes in moral and religious attitudes rather than changes in class structure.

At the moment, in a "permissive" society, the word "bloody," formerly regarded as the universal adjective of the "working man" or manual labourer (as exemplified by a television character, Alf Garnett) is used frequently in B.B.C. television and radio plays, presumably as a sign of emancipation from formerly held public standards. Its use would no longer be regarded as an indication of social class.

(c) Much the same might be said about *dress*. Dressing for dinner is no longer the invariable rule for the middle and upper classes, but slovenliness, laziness, or the desire to call attention to oneself may be the result of habit of a certain class; extreme measures taken to exhibit expensiveness of dress might indicate a desire to be regarded as a member of a class higher than that to which one belongs (*see also* VII, 12).

(d) Michael Argyle, in *Religious Behaviour* (Routledge and Kegan Paul, 1958), has suggested that social class influences religion rather than vice versa. It would seem that the middle and upper classes favour the Church of England rather than the nonconformist churches or the Catholic Church. The fluid position of social classes in Britain at the present day is such that the superiority of the Anglican Church may well be a historical rather than a contemporary influence. However, Margaret Stacey, in *Tradition and Change: A Study of Banbury* (Oxford University Press, 1960), found that in the Banbury district the gentry and aristocracy were usually Anglican; those who were not were Roman Catholic.

10. Leisure activities. The nature of the "affluent society" of recent years has blurred the lines which used to define class in terms of economic status and personal expenditure: formerly the poor spent what money they had on food and clothes, saving being the privilege of the middle class.

(a) The era of *high wages* has modified this simple pattern. Dr Mark Abrahams has remarked that the prosperity of the working class during the Second World War was expressed in their spending on beer, cigarettes and cinemas; in the 1950s, the emphasis fell on food, housing, fuel and light, household goods, private motoring and foreign travel.

(b) A change has occurred not only in quantity but also in *quality*: young working-class housewives today favour the more attractive foods and clothes, and are not so concerned about price.

(c) More people *read*, but the daily newspapers are still the major fare.

(d) *Sports* and club membership have been the subject of statistical investigation, but little light has been thrown on this aspect as far as membership of social class is concerned, although behaviour at sporting events is an obvious pointer to social class, and the various political and social clubs are usually well class-orientated.

(e) In *political voting* again, the allegiance of certain sections of the population is obvious, but the picture is complicated by such facts as that, *e.g.*, a trade unionist is not necessarily a Labour Party supporter, whilst a rich industrialist may well be, as will be the intellectual Socialist. In a Greenwich sample, M. Benney, A. P. Gray and R. H. Pear, in *How People Vote: A Study of Electoral Behaviour in Greenwich* (Routledge and Kegan Paul, 1956), found that subjective assessments, *i.e.* estimates made by people themselves of their social class seemed to show a strong relationship with voting behaviour.

11. Conclusion. It is an indication of the complexity of the modern problem of social classes, contrasted with the relative simplicity of classification in Victorian times, that the sociologist is apt to find himself a little self-conscious in discussing it. Not only may he himself be a member of the "new class" referred to in **3** (e) and so be a little diffident about commenting on his fellow-men, but the complex patterns of social structure have changed moral judgments and social attitudes since the experiences of two world wars and have made us less certain of what is "superior" or "inferior" in the details of our national life.

Despite the current "freedoms" of attitudes towards violence, crude language and sex behaviour, it may be suggested that the outstanding success of the B.B.C. television serial of Galsworthy's *Forsyte Saga* may indicate that many of the so-called "working class" regard the middle-class world of the Forsytes as an ideal, not as a relic of a bygone age. The cultured and bigoted Soames Forsyte, rather than the foul-mouthed and bigoted Alf Garnett, might well be the hero-figure of the drama of social classes.

PROGRESS TEST 9

1. What is the social environment of the modern family group? **(1–3)**

2. What were the "Two Nations" of the nineteenth century? **(2)**

3. What have been the broad effects of industrialisation on social class? **(3)**

4. Why has it become difficult to define "social class"? **(4)**

5. What may be suggested as the determinants of social class today? **(5)**

6. How valid is a classification of social classes based on income and occupation? **(6)**

7. What light does the consideration of educational facilities today throw on the determination of social class? **(7)**

8. What are the difficulties of using subjective assessments to determine social class? **(8)**

9. How are "ways of life" significant in indicating social class? **(9)**

10. What light does the consideration of ways of spending money and leisure and voting behaviour throw on the question of the determination of social class? **(10)**

11. Has the concept of an "ideal" middle class any validity? **(11)**

CHAPTER X

EDUCATION AND THE SOCIAL STRUCTURE

THE EDUCATIONAL BACKGROUND

1. The social significance of education. The social structure of a community can be determined by its own members only if they are aware of its nature and constitution, and if they are social beings (*see* I, **6**).

Plato's view was that education enables men and women to see things in their right proportion, to "see things whole." Where such knowledge and will to determine the social structure are lacking, the structure can be determined only by historical circumstances; individual persons will then be the victims of the social structure, not its architects, and their education will be regarded not as an end in itself, as part of the achieving of the "Good Life," but as a means used by others for the achieving of *their* ends.

2. The social purpose of education. If any kind of "ideal" social structure is to be attained—meaning by that a structure that will enable the members of the community to realise their potential talents and live as happy a life as is reasonably possible—then it should be the *purpose of education* to enable them to see the problems of their society in relation to their own personal problems and aspirations, actively to take a part in resolving those problems and to acquire such skills in mental and physical activity as will permit them to pursue those personal and social ends jointly and efficiently. "A healthy mind in a healthy body" was the ancient Greek ideal; a considerable amount of sociological discussion centres around the meaning of the expression "a healthy mind."

3. The basic tools of the educational process. The basic tools of human beings in their struggle to master their environment and their own "human nature" are reading, writing and

89

the acquisition of a facility with numbers — the "three R's" of the old-fashioned elementary school. All the philosophy and science of the modern world are elaborations of these basic tools, just as intricate machines are elaborations of the human hand and foot.

(a) The process of acquiring skills with these elaborations is a two-way development: it requires the receiving as well as the giving of knowledge, and demands effort from both the learner and the teacher.

(b) The success of such effort will depend on the ability to meet the demands of the skill studied: it seems that a special intelligence is necessary in the acquisition of certain kinds of knowledge as well as a general intelligence; e.g. it may be possible for a non-mathematically minded person to acquire a fair amount of mathematical knowledge, but the process will be much easier and probably much more fruitful for a person who has a gift for mathematics.

4. The progress of education in Britain. At the end of the nineteenth century there were about 20,000 public elementary schools, three-quarters of which were organised by religious or voluntary bodies. Secondary education was provided by the public schools and grammar schools, this education being related to the arts and humanities and reflecting the culture of a dominant class. There were endowed schools under the care of the Charity Commissioners. "Science" classes were held in various places and were supported by grants from the Science and Art Department. The universities of Oxford and Cambridge were the centre of higher academic life; Durham University was founded in 1832, and the University of London was established, at first only as an examining body, in 1836. The demands of the twentieth century, with the Industrial Revolution reaching a climax and the Western world advancing rapidly into a technological era, called for a transformation of the educational scene and a constant adjustment of the public provision for educational facilities. A social attitude very different from that of the Newcastle Committee, which had reported in 1861 that "universal education was neither attainable nor desirable," now prevails.

5. Educational reform. The main developments in the educational system have been as follows:

(*a*) A Board of Education was created in 1899, a *central government body* which subsequently became the Ministry of Education and, in the Labour administration which began in 1964, the Department of Education and Science.

(*b*) The *Education Act*, 1902, created local education authorities (the L.E.A.s), the county council and county borough councils, which could provide *secondary education*. The new grammar schools which had been built—some had become exclusive "public schools"—were invited to become "direct-grant" schools, providing for a certain number of free places, or "maintained" schools, *i.e.* maintained by the L.E.A.

(*c*) After 1905 junior *technical* schools were built, and were recognised in 1913 as secondary schools.

(*d*) The Hadow Report of 1926, *The Education of the Adolescent*, envisaged two types of secondary education.

(*i*) *Grammar school* education, with a school-leaving age of sixteen or over.

(*ii*) A more practically based education in the *secondary modern school*, with a leaving age of fourteen or over.

(*e*) Both the Spens Report of 1938 and the Norwood Report of 1943 rejected the idea of "multilateral schools," corresponding to what are now known as *"comprehensive schools."*

(*f*) The *Education Act* of 1944 replaced the previous classification of publicly aided education by a new classification into *primary*, *secondary* and *further education*, provided for the school-leaving age to be raised to fifteen and imposed upon local authorities the duty of ensuring that efficient education throughout the three stages should be available for all those of school age within their areas.

(*g*) In 1948 a system for the *General Certificate of Education* was introduced, and was followed in 1965 by the *Certificate of Secondary Education*, designed for pupils completing five years' secondary education but not taking the G.C.E. examinations at Ordinary Level.

(*h*) The Labour administration which began in 1964 endeavoured to convert some grammar schools into *comprehensive schools*; these steps were resisted by authorities representing populations with a large number of supporters of the grammar school system.

(*i*) Some of the extremist Labour M.P.s advocated the abolition of the public schools (or alternatively the provision of public schools for everybody); however, the public schools continue to flourish with support from all classes with sufficient financial resources.

NOTE

(*a*) At January 1970, the number of pupils in the schools in England and Wales were:

Total of full-time pupils   8,800,843
Pupils in maintained schools, exclud-
ing nursery and special schools:
           primary pupils   5,021,593
        secondary pupils   3,143,879

(*b*) The total expenditure by public authorities in England and Wales in 1969–70 on education and related items such as school meals and milk, maintenance grants and grants to students and the transport of pupils amounted to £1,979 million.   This was 160 per cent higher than in 1959–60; the comparison excludes effects of price increases as well as increases in real terms.   The biggest relative increases were in expenditure on tuition in teacher training, on grants to universities in England and Wales, and on further education, in this order.

Statistics of Education, 1971.

EDUCATION AND TECHNOLOGY

6. Education and science.   In Britain, economic and social factors have influenced public education, orientating it towards the demands of a commercial and industrial economy, and to the needs of an increasingly complex technology.   With a mass educational system, the breaking down of the old class system, the emergence of a new, lower professional class characterised by the proliferation of "qualifications" (*see* IX, **3** (*e*)) and an emphasis on examination results as evidence of competence in some branch of knowledge, which can be used by individuals, industrial organisations or the state in the pursuit of economic advantage, the pattern of education has changed to correspond with changes in the social structure itself and with new social attitudes towards the nature and purpose of education.

(*a*) In Britain, the *public schools* educated pupils for

leadership in public and professional life, and preserved a culture (using this word in the everyday sense) based on literary and artistic appreciation; the *grammar schools* educated the squirearchy and middle class generally; and the state *elementary schools* provided instruction sufficient in the "three Rs" to produce the clerks and mechanics.

(*b*) Increased technology and its use by the new capitalists as the Industrial Revolution continued necessitated the accumulation and exploitation of *scientific knowledge*. There came about the distinction between "pure" and "applied" science, based on the distinction between science pursued for its own sake and research, the ultimate aims of which are commercial and industrial exploitation and the building of armaments.

(*c*) Lord Snow, lecturing in 1961 on "Two Cultures and the Scientific Revolution," argued that science and technology have become as much a part of "culture" as the arts and the humanities; this would be so if science and technology had not become part of the economic and political complex, of which the main functions are noted in (*b*).

(*d*) The grammar schools have become bases of preparation for the *technological* as well as for the *traditional* professions based on the arts and the humanities, such as politics, the law and the Church.

7. The increasing emphasis on technology. The increasing international competition in technology for industry and for armaments between the wars resulted in technical education moving rapidly away from its lowly origins, financed by the "whisky money" (the compensation money originally intended for publicans deprived of their licences and used to finance twelve polytechnics in London, thirteen in the provinces and over one hundred science schools between 1890 and 1902). The original "mechanics' institutes" developed rapidly into technical colleges, courses in science subjects were formed and various examining bodies were created.

(*a*) The new *redbrick universities* (three of them were created between the wars) and the *university colleges*, which subsequently obtained university charters, enabling them to grant their own degrees, were overtaken by this technological development in that their objections to the giving of degree-granting powers to technological colleges, expressed in the deliberations of the Percy Committee which reported in 1945 on *Higher Technological Education*, were overridden by events.

(*b*) In 1956 the Government classified *technical colleges* into local colleges, area colleges, regional colleges and colleges of advanced technology, and in 1964 implemented proposals of the Robbins Committee, which had reported in 1963 on the pattern of full-time higher education in Great Britain, by setting up a Council for National Academic Awards. This Council announced in 1965 its intention to award first and higher degrees. Certain technological colleges became technological universities.

(*c*) Education can be said to have reached the stage corresponding to the organisation of society in the final stage of Rostow's "stages of economic growth" (*see* IV, **10**).

(*d*) The *Industrial Training Act*, 1964, provided for the establishment of industrial training boards to promote and supervise standards of training throughout industry. The system has been extended to cover non-technological workers, *e.g.* those in local government employment (*see* XIII, **4**).

NOTE

The number of students enrolled at grant-aided further education establishments in England and Wales in 1970 are given below. From 1 April 1965, the Colleges of Advanced Technology ceased to be further education establishments and received university status.

		Number of students, in thousands
Major establishments		
Full-time		237·8
Sandwich		36·5
Part-time day		784·7
of which		
Day release	627·9	
Evening only		736·4
Total major establishments		1,759·4
Evening institutes		1,421·8
Total in grant-aided establishments		3,181·2

These figures do not cover universities, colleges of education, colleges and institutions aided or maintained by government departments other than the Department of Education and Science (*e.g.* the Ministry of Defence) and college of music.

Universities.—In Great Britain in 1969–70 there were 219,506 full-time students (as compared with 211,488 in 1968–69).

Teacher training.—In October, 1970, there were 230 training establishments, 126 maintained by the local education authorities, 62 by voluntary bodies and 42 maintained by universities. There were 119,443 men and women students and 10,834 full-time teaching staff.

Statistics of Education.

CONFLICT IN EDUCATION

8. Conflict in the social and economic environment. The concentration of the educational systems of the Western world on the training of future workers rather than on the bringing out of the talents and potentialities of young people and on helping them through the strains and disturbances of adolescence has led to frustrations and deep unhappiness for millions of people who see themselves as fodder for industrial and commercial battles alien to their own desires and aspirations.

(*a*) Hence the student disturbances, manifest in the conflicts with authority, representing the old, settled social and economic order.

(*i*) The prospect of spending the greater part of their lives in a monotonous job, or at least as employees rather than participators in the social and economic environment, has been too appalling for some students to bear. The majority come to terms with the industrial and social complex; they become upholders of the rigidities of the social system in their turn.

(*ii*) Young people have neither the *maturity*, the *knowledge* nor the *technical ability* effectively to direct their efforts towards reform (*see also* IV, **17**). Dictators and war-leaders are well aware of the power of organisation over apathy and ignorance of the technicalities of government.

(*b*) The Vice-Chancellor of Nottingham University, in February 1969, commented on a fall in the percentage of schoolchildren studying *science*, a slackening in the demand for science places at the universities and a reluctance of young scientists to work in industry. It seems that the new disciplines like social science are more attractive. The difficulties of sociological science have been commented on earlier in this book (*see* I, **8**) and it should be clear by this time that knowledge of the nature of the social complex is not in itself a sufficient remedy for the world's problems.

9. Conflict in the school environment. Closer to a practical, or at least a more immediate, solution are the conflicts which arise in the narrower sphere of the school environment. The division between children of the "grammar school type" and children of the "secondary modern school type" has resulted in a conflict not so much in the children themselves as in society.

(*a*) The Labour Government accelerated the abolition of the "eleven plus" examination for entrance to secondary schools and initiated a campaign for "comprehensive schools," which met considerable resistance from some local authorities (*see* **5** (*e*) and (*h*)).

(*b*) A report of the Inner London Education Authority has shown that of a sample of 11,431 children admitted at eleven to comprehensive schools in 1960, 7,613 passed "O" Level G.C.E., though only 1,648 of them had been "grammar designated" in 1960. The evidence so far suggests that comprehensive schooling encourages a "levelling-up" process.

(*c*) There is considerable debate about the priorities to be given to those children who are especially intelligent.

(*d*) It seems that at school, as in life, a person aims to join his "peer group"—that group with abilities roughly equivalent to his own, of his own age group and, usually, of the same sex. Conflict will certainly arise if a person is forced by circumstances to live in a group which is not his "peer group" and thus not achieve the status, and play the corresponding role, which he desires (*see* VII, **12**, and Cyril Smith, *Adolescence* (Longmans, Green & Co., 1968)).

10. Education and the mass media. Education as a deliberate social process directed by a responsible authority is part of the education given by the experience of living; it is a form of communication between social beings. Communication includes the use of the mass media which are a part of the education of the child and the man and woman of the modern industrial world.

(a) The implementing of the *Education Act* of 1870, resulting in the emergence of a reading class (as distinct from a literary class), was followed by the founding of a "new journalism," aimed at providing popular exposition of the news, amusement and entertainment. The *Daily Mail* was founded in 1896 by Alfred Harmsworth, later Lord Northcliffe, and in 1904 he began to publish the *Daily Mirror* as a cheap paper for women.

(b) It was not long before a large part of the London and provincial press had become the property of several large *combines*. The Royal Commissions on the Press, 1947–9 and 1961–2, commented on the increasing concentration of ownership of the press.

(c) The cheap prices of modern newspapers depend on mass circulation and advertising.

(d) The British Broadcasting Company was formed in 1922 and was superseded by the British Broadcasting Corporation in 1927. Lord Reith was Director-General of the B.B.C. from 1927 to 1935 and insisted on high standards of taste and presentation. Standards subsequently declined, and television (of the possibilities of which Lord Reith, in a recent interview, pronounced himself "terrified") followed a popular trend, emphasised by the competition of commercial radio and television; when "pirate" radio broadcasting stations were banned in 1967, there was so much popular resentment that the B.B.C. provided its own "pop music" programmes.

NOTE: It is easy to be censorious about other people's entertainment; however, there can be no doubt about the *educative* value of much that is broadcast and televised.

11. Research into the mass media. It would seem that the mass media in themselves have little effect in comparison (and in competition) with the whole background of the education, training, mental ability and cultural group of the individual.

(a) There has been research into the effects of television (*e.g.* J. D. Halloran, *The Effects of Mass Communication with Special Reference to Television* (Leicester University

Press, 1964)). Some of the conclusions reached in investigations of this kind are a little confusing but some observers state that television reduces viewers' activities and initiative and others that it has a narcotic effect and that a genuinely critical outlook is restrained. However, it would seem that the effect of television depends on age, education, social class and intelligence.

(*b*) It appears that themes of sex and violence have had a damaging effect on delinquents and those with tendencies towards delinquency (*see* Halloran in (*a*) above).

In 1971 a new advisory group was set up by the B.B.C. to study the social effects of television, including the effects of violence in programmes.

(*c*) The publishing in a paper-back issue of D. H. Lawrence's *Lady Chatterley's Lover*, which was prosecuted in 1960 under the *Obscene Publications Act*, 1959, and the finding by the jury that the book was not obscene, seem to have loosed a spate of permissiveness, which has provoked a reaction, in the field of television, by an organisation founded by Mary Whitehouse. It is too early to judge the extent and depth of this phase or era of permissiveness; like student disturbances and riots, it seems to be prevalent among those temperamentally unable to accept norms hitherto socially accepted and among intellectuals struggling to be free from restraint; the remainder of the population retains its customary or occasional mild bawdiness.

12. Leisure and education. The way in which one spends one's leisure is both the result of and an influence on one's education (*see also* IX, **10**).

(*a*) Statistics indicate that with the increase of leisure arising from holidays with pay and the shortening of working hours, for the working class at least, there has been since the early 1950s an increasing participation in such *sports* as skiing, sailing, gliding, horse-riding and underwater sports, whilst the attendances at spectator sports such as horse-racing, greyhound-racing and football have declined.

(*b*) *Gambling*, however, especially in its working-class form of bingo, has increased. The total amount of money staked on organised betting and gambling has been estimated for 1969 to be £2,225 million (it was estimated at

£915 million for 1968).   About two-thirds of the money staked was on horse-racing.   The total amounts staked on bingo are, perhaps surprisingly, not large.   (*Britain: An Official Handbook* (H.M.S.O., 1969)).

A 1973 estimate was that 86 per cent of all British males spent over £2,000 million in over 15,000 betting offices and countless private betting pools.   An American observer commented that in Las Vegas, Nevada, mothers were feeding the family food money into the slot machines.

(*c*) Studies such as those made by, *e.g.*, Richard Hoggart in *The Uses of Literacy* (Chatto and Windus, 1957) and T. Carter and J. S. Downham in *The Communication of Ideas: A Study of Contemporary Influences on Urban Life* (Chatto and Windus, 1954), suggest that, though two-thirds of the population now have some form of holiday abroad, Ostend rather than Florence, and the Italian beaches rather than the Italian antiquities, are the visiting-places of the newly leisured people.

PROGRESS TEST 10

1. What is the social significance of education?   (**1**)

2. What is the social purpose of education?   (**2**)

3. What are the basic tools of the educational process?   (**3**)

4. Review the main stages of publicly provided education in Britain.   (**4, 5**)

5. What place has science taken in the provision of education? (**6, 8** (*b*))

6. What have been the main features of technological instruction and development?   (**7**)

7. What has been a major source of conflict in the social and economic environment?   (**8**)

8. What has been a major source of conflict in the school environment?   (**9**)

9. What is the significance of a "peer group"?   (**9** (*d*))

10. What has been the general development of the mass media? (**10**)

11. Has it been possible to ascertain the effects of the mass media on social behaviour?   (**11**)

12. What has been the relationship between increased leisure and education in Britain?   (**12**)

CHAPTER XI

RELIGION AND MORAL STANDARDS

RELIGION AND MORALS IN THE SOCIAL STRUCTURE

1. Education and religion. The organisation of Christianity and the teachings of the Christian Church exerted a strong influence on the social structure of the Western world. The Church and the state were the twin institutions of the Middle Ages, the Church fulfilling the function of a poor-law authority. The Reformation and the dissolution of the monasteries and the increasing scope of the powers of the state tended to weaken the bonds between the family structure and the religious and moral life (*see* VIII, **6** and IX, **9** (*d*)).

(*a*) Religion as a body of organised beliefs and practices binding society together (the word religion is derived from Latin *religare*, to bind) remained a *powerful force*. In the upper classes, a gentleman was essentially a *Christian* gentleman. In nineteenth-century industrial Britain, religion was not considered incompatible with capitalism; humility, patience, obedience to one's superiors and a willingness to put up with the miseries of this life in the belief that they would be compensated for in the next were held to be the cardinal virtues of the labouring classes (*see also* XIII, **6**).

(*b*) There was, however, *conflict* between the major religious bodies during the dispute between the Crown and Parliament in the Civil Wars, which culminated in the triumph of the Puritans and the rule of the country by a military dictatorship for eleven years (1649–60). Until 1870 the antagonism between the Church of England and the nonconformist churches frustrated attempts to found a system of national elementary education (*see* X, **4**).

(*c*) Educational discussions had been concerned with ensuring that religious worship in publicly financed schools was non-denominational; the *Education Act* of 1944 made a non-denominational service compulsory in the schools (sections 25 and 26).

2. Religion as a form of social control.   It is evident that religion has been one of the forms of social control—the other main form is the law.   Attempts by different religious groups at controlling and destroying the religious beliefs and practices of others, or compelling comformity by means of torture and executions, must fail because religion has its base in the human personality.

(*a*) Totalitarian régimes are apt to try to suppress religious freedom, because they regard the Church as a state within a state.   Communism in the U.S.S.R. could not succeed in destroying organised religion.

(*b*) Napoleon I as First Consul was wise enough to seek a religious settlement with the Pope (1801 and 1802); he permitted religious freedom while upholding the authority of the state.

(*c*) In Italy, Roman Catholicism is not merely *a* religion, it is *the* religion of the people; yet Italy has one of the largest Communist Parties in Europe.

(*d*) Religious freedom is a stronger binding force than religious oppression, for it is social control freely embraced and, although moral standards can exist apart from a religious organisation (*e. g.* in the case of the humanists), the acceptance of those standards is in itself a binding social force, similar to that of religion.

(*e*) Where standards of morality have been closely allied to religious observance in a society, and the bases of that religious observance have been destroyed, then conflict and confusion occur in that society, and moral values are affected.

3. The effects of scientific advancement.   Before the end of the nineteenth century advances in science had shaken established belief in Britain.

(*a*) The work of *Georges Cuvier* (1769–1832) in comparative anatomy, of *Charles Lyell* (1795–1895) in geology, and of *Charles Darwin* (1809–82) and *Alfred Russel Wallace* (1823–1913) on natural selection pointed to a new view of the origin of man and his place in the universe. It began a controversy of science versus religion, which today seems irrelevant to the discussion of the relation between religion and science, and particularly irrelevant to a discussion of the relation between morality and science; morality is a matter for social science, not natural science.

(b) The impact of two world wars and of the economic chaos of the inter-war and post-war period was reinforced by the impact of great technological advances; both tended to undermine the authority of the churches in their claim to the spiritual and social leadership of the nation. In addition, the developments in birth-control techniques tended to weaken the control of the churches.

4. The decline in the influence of organised religion. There has been a decline in the influence of organised religion, at least as far as the established Church of England is concerned. The recruiting of "pop" groups to liven up church services, and the hesitancy shown by clergy to denounce what would once have been regarded as serious sins, convey the impression that the churches wish to *woo* rather than to *command* allegiance, and the ecumenical movement, the call to unity, indicates a closing of the ranks of the hitherto divided denominations in opposition to the general apathy to organised religion.

(a) *Statistical* investigation confirms this impression.

(i) The *Church of England Year Book* for 1936 showed that during 1936 the number of confirmations had decreased by nearly 15,000, and the number of Sunday School teachers by nearly 6,000.

(ii) More recent statistics *confirm* the existence of this trend: studies of church attendance in York have shown a decline from 25 per cent in 1900 to 14 per cent in 1948 (M. Argyle, *Religious Behaviour* (Routledge and Kegan Paul, 1958)), and similarly in Oxford (J. M. Mogey, *Family and Neighbourhood* (Oxford University Press, 1956)).

(iii) A 1957 Gallup poll revealed considerable discrepancies between church membership and church attendance, except for Roman Catholics. A recent Gallup poll showed that of the Roman Catholics interviewed, 59 per cent said that they went to church regularly, but only 23 per cent said that they had attended the previous Sunday. Of the 78 per cent of the population believing in God, only 11 per cent of the men and 16 per cent of the women went to church. The age group of those under twenty showed less religious conviction than other age groups.

(v) In about 1900, the "nonconformist conscience" was an important influence in British religious life, which was largely under *Methodist* leadership. In 1907 there were 904,852 Methodist members, but by 1969 the number had decreased to 724,892, and there were less than half as many Methodist Sunday Schools as there had been at their height in the nineteenth century. The proposed union of Methodists with Anglicans (John Wesley was an Anglican all his life) seem to indicate, at least to some extent, an attempt at unity.

(b) No doubt such events can be paralleled in all ages of history. Corresponding to the sects of the ancient world are the sects of the modern world, particularly in the U.S.A. The *success* of popular evangelists like Dr Billy Graham seems to indicate a desire for a religious experience which is not satisfied by the established, organised churches.

CHANGES IN MORAL STANDARDS

5. The decline in moral standards. Accompanying the decline in the prestige and influence of organised religion has been a decline in standards of moral behaviour. The use of the word "decline," in what is attempting to be a dispassionate study, is justified by a term in current use, "permissiveness," which implies a decline.

(a) It is very difficult to describe clearly what is meant by "a decline in the moral standards" with reference to present-day society, when one considers the cruelty, licentiousness and depravity of previous ages and periods, from the barbarities of Roman days to the horrors suffered by the labouring classes during the Industrial Revolution in the nineteenth century. Apart from the Nazi phase in Germany, there appears to have been a *heightening* of social consciousness in Europe, a reaching towards a conception of "human rights"; there is a lessening of inequality of income, a spread of educational facilities and a dissatisfaction with social conditions, which in itself is the expression of the desire for a better "civilisation" (in the sense in which this term has been used in IX, **4** (b)).

(b) Side by side with complaints of the depravities and excesses of youth are the reports of such organisations as the Outward Bound Trust, formed to foster personal integrity and offer service to the community. There is a *Standing Conference of National Voluntary Youth Organisations*, to which twenty-seven of the largest voluntary youth organisations belong, each with at least 10,000 members between the ages of ten and twenty-one.

(c) Faced with a multitude of details of facts referring not only to standards in this era but also to standards over the vast panorama of history, the sociologist considering moral standards is advised, unless he is another Comte or Spencer or Westermarck, to confine his studies to matters of current discussion on a limited scale, such as those which are dealt with in the following sections.

6. Sexual morality. It might be suggested that there has never been an age in which people were so preoccupied with sexual relations than the present, if it were not for the suspicion, founded upon a study of the literature, habits and customs of previous ages, and upon a study of the ways in which the population of the world has been increasing (*see* XV, **4**), that sex has been a major preoccupation in other ages, too. While observing in passing that the word "morality" is often interpreted as meaning "sexual morality," we had better confine ourselves to the statistical statements which may be taken to illustrate the probable or, at least, the possible effects of those factors considered in **3** and **4** above, operating in recent social life.

7. Illegitimacy.

(a) The National Council for the Unmarried Mother reported in September 1967 that the number of schoolgirl mothers was to be expected to rise when the school-leaving age was raised to sixteen. In 1947 girls of fifteen and under who had illegitimate babies numbered 204; in 1957, 299; in 1967, 1,240; in 1969, nearly 1,500.

(b) During the ten years previous to 1967, illegitimate births had more than doubled: the figure for teenage mothers rose from 5,500 to 19,500. One-third of illegitimate births were to married women.

(c) The Registrar-General's report in 1972 showed that there was a fall in the number of illegitimate children compared with the peak year of 1967; but the proportion was still far higher than ten years previously. In 1961 illegitimate births formed 5·8 per cent of all births, and in 1970 8·2 per cent (the birth rate in 1970 continued the decline begun in 1965). There were 64,744 children born outside marriage and a further 70,623 were conceived before the parents married. 1,425 children were borne by girls under sixteen; four of them to girls under eleven.

In 1969 in England and Wales, every sixth child was conceived out of marriage; in 1970, every twelfth child was illegitimate. In Scotland there has been a steady increase during the last ten years in the percentage of illegitimate births: in 1960, 4·35 per cent, in 1969, 7·45 per cent—the figures for Glasgow are 1960, 5·3 per cent, 1969, 10·7 per cent.

(d) In the U.S.A., over 300,000 illegitimate babies are born every year—1 in 14 births. Illegitimate births have trebled since 1940. If there is a continuation of present trends, the proportion of illegitimate births will be 1 in 10 in the 1970s. About 44 per cent of the unmarried mothers are under twenty. Welfare officials have reported that 50 per cent of the women having illegitimate children have one or more illegitimate children subsequently. The big cities have the highest illegitimacy rate—1 in 6 babies in New York.

NOTE: The basic measures of illegitimacy are number, ratio and rate. The *number* of illegitimate births is the total volume and is used to compute both the ratio and the rate. The illegitimate *ratio* is the number of illegitimate births per 1,000 live births. Relatively few illegitimate births among young females will result in a very high illegitimacy ratio for the group because of the small number of total live births to females in the group. The illegitimacy *rate* is the number of illegitimate births per 1,000 unmarried females of child-bearing age; and it is this measure which indicates whether illegitimacy is increasing or decreasing. (*See* "Teen-Age Unwed Mothers in American Society," Clark E. Vincent, *Journal of Social Issues*, 1966, XXII, No. 2, pp. 24, 25). One must be careful, therefore, not to use the ratio measure to "prove" assertions about the sex habits of teenagers.

(e) A French sociologist, Gilbert Dooghe, stated in a report in 1968 that only 59 per cent of all first births in France could be considered as conceived in marriage.

(f) In 1969, 35 per cent of brides in West Germany were pregnant at the time of their marriage; 45,498 children were born to unmarried parents—an illegitimacy ratio of 50. In East Germany in 1970, the illegitimacy ratio was 130—130 births out of every 1,000 took place outside marriage.

(g) The Dutch Central Bureau of Statistics shows that in the period 1960–66 four out of five women who were married below the age of 20 were pregnant on their wedding day. In the 20–24 year old age group, the figure was 25 per cent.

(h) In Denmark in 1964, 9·3 per cent of all births were illegitimate; in 1969, 11·3.

(i) In Norway, in 1969, of the 64,746 children born, 4,163 were illegitimate—a rate of 6 per cent.

(j) The Swedish Year Book shows that in 1971 22 per cent of all children born were illegitimate. A Swedish researcher, Birgitta Linner, has reported that in Sweden more than 40 per cent of all firstborn babies are conceived before the wedding takes place.

(k) In a survey by the National Foundation for Educational Research and the National Children's Bureau, published in 1971, it is revealed that the chances of a successful early life are "heavily loaded" against the illegitimately born child; by contrast, it would seem that adopted children fare even better than legitimate children (*Born Illegitimate, Social and Educational Implications*, National Foundation for Educational Research in England and Wales). The Technical Director of the Observation Centre for Juvenile Delinquents in Paris, Dr. Paul La Maol, stated recently that illegitimate children are more accident-prone, are more liable to illness and have a greater infant mortality rate than those born in wedlock.

8. Abortions.

(a) Between 27th April, 1968 (when abortions became legal) and the end of the year, 22,256 abortions were carried out in Britain. The annual report of the Department of Health and Social Security, published in August 1971, gave a figure of 80,723 legal abortions carried out in

England in 1970, an increase of more than 28,000 over the
1969 figure. The 83,851 for England and Wales included
39,532 single women, including 1,791 under 16. Fifty-five
per cent of the 1970 abortions were carried out in National
Health hospitals. Provisional figures for 1971 showed that
there were 21,879 notified therapeutic abortions, compared
with 15,020 in 1970; 47 per cent of the abortions were for
unmarried women. The Registrar-General's quarterly return showed that in the last quarter of 1971 38,000 women
in England and Wales, including 808 girls under 16, had
abortions—the equivalent of an annual rate of more than
150,000, as compared with the 86,565 for the whole of 1970.

(b) In the three months up to December 1968, 9,907
women had legal abortions in England and Wales; of this
number, 251 were girls under sixteen. In 1971, the chairman of the Brook Advisory Centre, running thirteen
contraceptive advice clinics in England and Scotland, said
that the growing number of pregnancies in schoolgirls was
causing concern. Nearly 1,500 girls under sixteen had
babies in 1969, and more than 1,200 had legal abortions—
giving a total of at least 2,700 girls pregnant before they
reached sixteen.

(c) Of the 22,256 cases noted in (a) for 1968, 47 per cent
were single women; about 17 per cent were under twenty;
and over 12,000 operations were carried out in London,
which by 1969 had attained, apparently, notoriety as an
abortion city for foreigners.

(d) The Minister for the Social Services, speaking to the
Family Planning Association in London in June 1969, said
that the abortion law itself was essentially a measure of
failure; he wanted a situation in which family planning was
so much a part of life that abortion was unnecessary. He
hoped to provide "comprehensive family planning" in the
future within the Health Service (see VIII, 11 (a)).

9. Sexually transmitted diseases. This term is now replacing the former expression "venereal diseases": this is perhaps
itself an indication of changed attitudes, for it tends to make
these diseases more "respectable," and encourage sufferers to
deal with their problem less furtively.

(a) According to the M.P. moving the second reading of
his Venereal Diseases Bill in March 1969 (to compel the

medical examination and treatment of persons suspected
to be suffering from V.D.), venereal disease has reached
epidemic proportions. In Britain every day 200 people
contract a venereal disease. It was estimated that 1 out of
every 300 people would attend V.D clinics in 1969 in Britain.
In 1967, 119,545 men and 56,829 women attended clinics.

(b) Promiscuity among the young has resulted in a steep
rise in the incidence of V.D. in the fifteen to twenty-four age
group. In 1967, 17,890 in this group attended clinics.

In 1967 there were 45,000 cases of gonorrhoea in Britain—
a 12 per cent rise since the previous year. One-third of the
gonorrhoea cases were among people under twenty-four.
More girls contracted the disease than boys.

(c) In 1969, some 140,000 cases of sexually transmitted
diseases were notified in Britain. These included 3,000
cases of syphilis, 55,000 of gonorrhoea and 74,000 of the
less serious non-specific urethritis.

Professor E. W. Walls, Professor of Anatomy and Dean of
the Faculty of Medicine in London University, stated in
April 1971 that in 1970 new cases of venereal diseases in
England and Wales exceeded 250,000 for the first time—one
person in every 200 of the population was known to have
become infected during the previous twelve months.

In his annual report for 1970, Sir George Godber, Chief
Medical Officer of the Department of Health and Social
Security, stated that the figures for 1970 were the highest
for a quarter of a century. There were 53,525 new cases of
gonorrhoea; the disease occurred most frequently among men
aged 20–24 and women aged 18–19. Though the number of
cases in children was still relatively small, the increase over
the last few years, especially in girls, gave cause for alarm.

(d) In the U.S.A., according to the *Wall Street Journal* of
September 9th 1968, the head of the venereal disease programme at the National Communicable Disease Centre
warned that gonorrhoea was out of control, and some
medical men have indicated that the disease has become
resistant to penicillin. There were 15,000 cases of syphilis
and 1,500,000 of gonorrhoea in 1967. In 1972 there were
two million cases of venereal disease; homosexuals accounted
for nearly one-fifth of the reported cases. It has been
estimated that in the U.S.A., someone contracts venereal
disease every twelve seconds. Dr. Geoffrey Simmons, of the

Los Angeles County Health Department, has predicted that by 1975 annual cases in the U.S.A. would rise to five million.

(e) In Europe in 1967 there were 500,000 cases of syphilis and five million of gonorrhoea.

(f) There is no doubt that promiscuity has been the prime cause in the rise of the incidence of venereal diseases.

10. Drugs.   Drug addiction has become a recent phenomenon.

(a) In 1961 there were only 471 known addicts in Britain, only two of whom were under twenty.   By the end of 1966, narcotic addiction had risen to 1,400.   Between 1961 and 1966, narcotic addiction trebled: heroin addiction increased sevenfold, especially among those under twenty.   The number of registered drug addicts fell by 36 to 1,430 in 1970; but in 1971 there were 1,555 registered addicts of hard drugs.   In 1969, 6,911 people were sentenced for drug offences and 9,000 in 1970, when there were 2,800 more cannabis convictions.   Almost 8,000 people were prosecuted in 1971 for unlawful possession of cannabis, a non-addictive drug.

The *Dangerous Drugs Act*, 1965, was passed to deal with professional drug trafficking offences.

(b) In the U.S.A., marijuana ("pot"), in its various forms, has come to be considered a serious threat to social stability by the World Health Organisation and the American Medical Association.   Juvenile arrests on marijuana charges rose by 3,433 per cent in California during the eight years to 1969.   This drug has a definite connection with anti-social, criminal behaviour, at least according to law enforcement agencies, who also maintain that its use leads to addiction to the hard narcotics, generally derived from opium.

(c) According to a recent United Nations report, world addiction to the hard narcotics numbers several hundred thousand.   India has reported 340,000 addicts; Hong Kong, 15,000; West Germany, 4,357; and Spain, 1,588.

11. Conclusion.   It is usual for the older generation to look askance at the moral standards and general behaviour of the young; in modern Western societies the older generation still adheres to the old moral standards, whilst the young, or a vocal, exhibitionist and provocative section of the young, appear to despise those values. Of Western society as a whole, it seems that there is scant regard for those virtues which in the ancient Roman republic were held to be most conducive to the worth of the citizen and the stability of the state: *pietas* (loyalty to the state, to those in authority and to the idea of social stability); *gravitas* (seriousness of purpose); and *dignitas* (conduct worthy of a given serious situation). Contempt for these virtues helped to destroy the Roman Empire.

Recent Gallup polls ascertained that 80 per cent of the people of the U.S.A. believed that morals were getting "worse", whilst only 10 per cent believed that they were getting better, compared with only 50 per cent of the people in 1961 who believed that morals were getting worse. In Europe, it was concluded that religious beliefs were declining, morals had slumped, honesty was on the wane and happiness and peace of mind were becoming rarer to find (*Sunday Telegraph*, 21st July 1968). The situation would be more serious if people were not aware of moral standards at all.

In 1968 the Pope's encyclical on contraception caused distress and unhappiness among many Catholics, brought face to face with the conflict between their desires and the teachings of their Church. That the encyclical was discussed widely among Protestants confronted with no such dilemma is evidence of the concern with moral standards which do not cease to be public standards even if they are disregarded by many individuals.

PROGRESS TEST 11

1. What is the connection between education and religion? **(1)**

2. Why is religion a form of social control? **(1, 2)**

3. What have been the effects on religious orthodoxy of scientific advances? **(3)**

4. What evidence is there for saying that there has been a decline in the prestige and influence of organised religion? **(4)**

5. Has there been a decline in "moral standards"? **(5)**

6. What is the evidence of a "low" sexual morality in Europe and the U.S.A.? **(6–9)**

7. What evidence is there of increasing drug addition in

Europe and the U.S.A.? **(10)**

    8. Is there still concern with the problem of "moral standards"? **(11)**

CHAPTER XII

CRIME AND DELINQUENCY

CRIME

1. The nature of crime.   An increase in crime may be the result of a decline in moral standards in a society, but a crime has a definite connotation.   Current moral standards may be in opposition to the law, *e.g.* drug-taking and drug-passing, and are in opposition to what the law-abiding section of the population regards as the best moral standards, and a moralist may suggest that murder and arson are but examples of supremely bad manners.   However, the law is not concerned with philosophic speculations, as any traffic warden will tell an erring motorist.

A *crime* is an offence against the laws of a country, punishable by the state, representing the judicial authority of the community, the nature of the punishment being determined by the judiciary in accordance with the laws, and administered through the apparatus of the police and prison system (*see* VII, **8** (*b*)).

(*a*) Offences against the laws are of two kinds:

(*i*) *Indictable, i.e.* to be tried by jury.
(*ii*) *Non-indictable, i.e.* to be disposed of summarily by a magistrate or a Justice of the Peace.

(*b*) The less serious indictable offences may be tried summarily at a magistrates' court if the accused consents; *i.e.* he may agree to be tried summarily or elect to go before a jury at the Crown Court.

(*c*) Most criminal cases (about 90 per cent) are decided by courts of summary jurisdiction.   The impression that may be given by the more sensational newspapers that the nation contains a large proportion of homicidal maniacs or sexually obsessed perverts is to be distrusted: most people live respectable lives.

2. Punishment. Theories of punishment relate to the following:

(*a*) *Retribution.* Suffering is imposed by the community on a guilty person on the principle of "an eye for an eye," as an act of revenge.

(*b*) *Deterrence.* The punishment inflicted is such as would deter would-be offenders from committing a similar crime, so that the community protects itself against the projected misdeeds of the criminally inclined.

(*i*) There is, however, an element of *retribution* in deterrence.

(*ii*) In the current controversy as to whether the abolition of *capital punishment* has or has not encouraged murder, statistics are used by both sides to support their case. The police are inclined to favour strong deterrence in the prevention of crime.

(*c*) *Reparation.* The criminal, as far as is possible, is made to make reparation for his crime. Recent legislation attempts to compensate victims of crimes of violence. On the side of the criminal, it is hoped that remorse will so affect him that he will attempt to repair the damage done to the fabric of society by his misdeeds.

(*d*) *Reformation.* This theory in which the criminal is induced to forsake his criminal ways and re-enter society as a law-abiding and useful citizen is closely allied to reparation. "Open prisons," reformatory régimes and organisations for the care of released prisoners are the practical expression of this view.

3. Society and crime. Philosophers, social reformers, those dismissed by the general epithet of "do-gooders" and upholders of stern discipline may dispute on their respective points of view. All their views and practices make up sociology. Theoretical explanations of the causes of crime have been many and various, from the works of Cesare Lombroso (1836–1919), who discussed the physical and psychical characteristics of what may be called a "criminal type," to theories of role, status and lack of opportunity or ability to realise goals (*see* VII, **12**) and to theories of anomie and conflict (*see* IV, **16, 17**). In this HANDBOOK we are concerned with the facts of recent trends in the social structure, again presenting the statistical facts as pointers to those trends, while remembering that trends may be reversed as societies achieve a "dynamic equilibrium" (*see* IV, **17**) and take measures to remove centres of strain in the social fabric.

4. Crime in modern Britain. David C. Marsh, in *The Changing Social Structure of England and Wales, 1871–1961* (Routledge and Kegan Paul, 1965), has given an excellent analysis of the changing pattern of crime in Britain.

A feature of the modern world has been the widening of the range of technical and scientific devices available to both the police and the criminal. The death and injury figures for road accidents indicate that a lethal instrument has been placed in the hands of the ordinary citizen, who finds himself liable to a host of prosecutions—in 1961 traffic offences accounted for by far the highest number of non-indictable offences (712,584 out of a total of 970,180, charges for drunkenness reaching 71,614). The broad trends which emerge from a study of the statistics appear to be as follows:

(*a*) There was a large *increase* in the number of indictable offences since 1900, and between 1951 and 1961, particularly offences against the person and against property, with or without violence (the latter word is used in a technical sense).

However, the statistics (and others of a similar nature) show only those reported to the police, for many offences have probably *not been reported*; it seems that the rush of modern life tends to induce many people to avoid any proceedings or complications, especially where a court proceeding is involved, which will involve them in trouble or loss of time. Motorists try to avoid losing a no-claims bonus, and many women would be embarrassed by reporting a sexual offence.

(*b*) The *major* group of known indictable offences concerned offences against *property* with violence, but they declined as a proportion of all indictable offences.

(*c*) The number of known offences against the *person* increased, of which *sexual* offences formed the greatest number.

(*i*) The Department of Criminal Science of the University of Cambridge has stated recently that "the number of persons brought before the courts on sexual charges has reached proportions hitherto unknown in the criminal records of this country."

(*ii*) Homosexual offences and prostitution have also been the subject of investigation.

(*iii*) Nevertheless, in 1961, sexual offences represented less than 3 per cent of all indictable offences known to the police.

(*iv*) The worst increase for twelve years in crimes of violence against the person was revealed by Home Office figures published in December, 1971. Covering the first nine months of 1971, they showed that the number of offences of this type known to the police rose to 34,426 from 30,186 in the same period of 1970—an average of 92 people per day in England and Wales were victims of violent crime. From 1963 onwards there has been an average increase of about 8·7 per cent. There was a 2·3 per cent drop in sexual offences from 18,192 to 17,770.

(*d*) A far greater number of *males* have been found guilty of indictable offences than females; in 1961, 158,717 males were charged and 23,500 females. But in 1970 there was a large increase in the number of women and girls convicted of indictable offences: the total of 39,161 was 12·8 per cent up on the 1968 figure. The increase among men and boys was 9·9 per cent, bringing the total to 244,664.

(*e*) Since 1938, the majority of persons found guilty of indictable offences have been under thirty years of age: of the male percentage of 87 in 1961, 67 per cent were under thirty. Of the total of 39,161 for 1970 given in (*d*) above, the biggest percentage increase was in the age group 21–29: 22·5 per cent.

(*f*) It would appear that suspended prison sentences have had little deterrent effect. In 1968, 32,002 people received suspended sentences; 4,688 committed further offences in the same year; and in 1969 10,473 of the 32,002 committed offences. (*See* 2 above.)

(*g*) The increase of violent crime in recent years has caused considerable disquiet. During the last twenty years, the prison population has doubled—in 1971, there was a record number of 40,070. The Home Office has warned that there have been no signs of any reversal of the increase of crime since the Second World War. There were 21,307 cases of violence in the first six months of 1971— 2,515 more than in the same period of 1970: 117 men, women and children were victims of violent crime every day.

(h) The *Criminal Justice Act*, 1972, provides three principal alternatives to imprisonment other than those existing: day training centres, "community service" work, and bail hostels. But the courts have been given powers to pass tougher sentences on offenders; *e.g.* gunmen face life imprisonment.

JUVENILE CRIME

5. Juvenile delinquency. The difficulty of interpreting crime statistics, due to the technical distinctions and descriptions involved (*e.g.* "violence" may be used to describe what the average person regards as a trivial act), will deter the wary sociologist from rushing to the conclusion that we have become more degenerate as a nation. However, the tendencies relating to offences by young people are too obvious to be overlooked or ignored, though it must always be remembered that since the Second World War there has been an increasing emphasis on the detection and prosecution of young offenders who in former days might have received the traditional "clip across the ear," and no legal action would have been taken.

(a) The number of young persons between the ages of 8 and 17 found guilty of indictable offences in England and Wales rose from about 28,000 in 1938 to over 64,000 in 1961.

(b) As a proportion of all persons found guilty of indictable offences, those of young persons under 17 formed 37 per cent in 1938, 36 per cent in 1951 and 35 per cent in 1961.

(c) As a proportion of *all* boys and girls in the age groups 8–14 and 14–17, the proportion found guilty of indictable offences has increased substantially—from 136 per 100,000 in 1938 to 452 in 1961 (see David C. Marsh, *The Changing Social Structure of England and Wales, 1871–1961* (Routledge and Kegan Paul, 1965)).

(d) Of the *non-indictable* offences, traffic offences (obstruction, nuisance, offences with pedal cycles, etc.) have increased since the 1930s, and form a considerable proportion of the total.

(e) The total number of juveniles found guilty of indictable offences in 1960 in England and Wales was 57,360; in

1970, 74,397; the figures for non-indictable offences are 1969; 49,640; 1970, 48,769.

6. The treatment of juvenile offenders. The crude and cruel methods of dealing with delinquent children in the nineteenth century—Parkhurst was established in 1838 for boys between the ages of eight and fifteen awaiting transportation at fifteen—aroused the public conscience, also stirred by the efforts of philanthropists and reformers like Robert Raikes, John Pounds, Robert Owen and Dr Barnado. By the twentieth century the social consequences of the *laissez-faire* attitude to juvenile offences received some attention and in 1907 borstals, or juvenile reformatories, were introduced.

(*a*) The *Children's Act*, 1908, provided that child offenders were to be tried in special juvenile courts, with the parents present.

(*b*) The *Children and Young Persons Act*, 1933, linked parent or guardian neglect with child delinquency. It defined a child as a person under the age of fourteen and a young person as one from the age of fourteen to seventeen. Those responsible for cruelty or neglect could be prosecuted, and children "in need of care and protection" could be removed from the custody of their parents or guardians. Such children could be placed under the care of a probation officer (the probation service was established in 1907) or could be sent to an "approved school." In future, the emphasis was to lie on rehabilitation and reform of juvenile offenders.

7. The Ingleby Report, 1960. The Ingleby Report, 1960, reviewed the law relating to young offenders and the means of education and training available to the courts. It recommended the following:

(*a*) The raising of the age of criminal responsibility to twelve years.

(*b*) The introduction of a unified system for dealing with children "in need of care and protection."

(*c*) The abolition of imprisonment for young persons under seventeen.

NOTE

(*i*) The *Criminal Justice Act*, 1961, gave effect to the last two recommendations: no person under seventeen may be sent to prison, but a fine may be imposed.

(*ii*) The *Children and Young Persons Act*, 1963, simplified the law relating to approved schools, and raised the age of criminal responsibility in England and Wales from eight to ten.

8. Penalties for juvenile offenders. The government department in England and Wales responsible for the treatment of offenders is the Home Office. Offenders under seventeen are tried in the juvenile courts, and those between seventeen and twenty-one in the ordinary courts. An offender of any age may be placed under the care of a probation officer.

(*a*) First offenders may be ordered to attend at an *attendance centre*.

(*b*) *Detention centres* are used for discipline extending over three to six months, with a subsequent period of compulsory supervision.

(*c*) *Remand centres* are used for the detention of persons between seventeen and twenty-one remanded or committed in custody for trial or sentence.

(*d*) *Remand homes* are used for the safe custody of juveniles before their appearance in court, for detention after committal to an approved school or for a detention of one month.

(*e*) *Approved schools* are boarding schools supervised by the Home Office; the system has been criticised on the ground that it results in the compulsory association of unfortunate or neglected children with criminal offenders.

(*f*) *Borstal training* is carried out at institutions conducted on a public-school "house" system; it is imposed on persons aged between fifteen and twenty-one committed on an indictment for an offence punishable by imprisonment.

NOTE: See *The Treatment of Offenders in Britain* (Central Office of Information), Pamphlet 35, and *Children in Britain*, Pamphlet 34.

9. Recent White Papers and legislation. The general spirit in legislation relating to young offenders has been to prevent juvenile crime and to consider the welfare of young people.

(a) The *Children and Young Persons Act*, 1963, which defined a "child" as being a person under the age of eighteen, stated that it is the duty of every local authority to make available such advice, guidance and assistance as might promote the welfare of children by diminishing the need to receive children into care or keep them in care or to bring children before a juvenile court.

(b) In August 1965, the Government published a White Paper, *The Child, the Family and the Young Offender* (Cmnd. 2742), in which it was noted that a high proportion of adult criminals had been juvenile offenders, "so that every advance in dealing with the young offender helps also in the attack on adult crime" (para. 4). It was proposed to remove young people as far as possible from the jurisdiction of the court, and to empower each local authority, through its children's committee, to appoint *Family Councils* of social workers to deal with each case involving those under sixteen, as far as possible in consultation and agreement with the parents. If agreement with the parents proved impossible, or the case was of sufficient gravity, the case would be referred to a *Family Court*, a special magistrates' court, which would also act as a young offenders' court for persons aged between sixteen and twenty-one.

The proposals met with considerable criticism, and were modified as below.

(c) In the White Paper of April, 1968, *Children in Trouble* (Cmnd. 3601), the proposal for Family Councils was dropped.

(i) It was proposed that *social workers* would deal with young offenders.

(ii) *Juvenile courts* would be retained, and seventeen would remain as the upper age limit for the trying of young offenders in juvenile courts.

(iii) The approved school system and similar *punishment by detention* would be abolished.

(iv) The *local authorities* would be given increased responsibilities for the care of offenders.

10. The Children and Young Persons Act, 1969. This Act followed the principles of *Children in Trouble*. It provided for help to be given to the parents of deprived and delinquent children, all children, as far as possible, being regarded as equal before the law. Criminal proceedings, except for homicide, have been abolished against children under 14 and proceedings against persons between 14 and 17 are restricted. A child of 10 or over can still be found guilty of a crime, but he cannot be found guilty of an offence; that is to say, a child can be guilty of a crime without an offence being formulated against him.

Approved schools and remand homes will be replaced by "community homes," probation will be replaced by supervision and the "fit person" order will be replaced by a "care order." Detention will be limited to special circumstances, where it is necessary for the protection of the public.

Thus, almost the entire responsibility for dealing with juvenile offenders is now placed on the local authority, which has the duty of bringing an offender before the court and looking after him if he is committeed to its care.

Since J.P.s no longer have the power to send young offenders to approved schools, they have preferred to send them to a detention centre or a borstal rather than take the risk of an offender being given his liberty. (The number of juveniles in borstal institutions jumped by 25 per cent between 1970 and 1971.) There have been, in fact, some criticisms by magistrates of the operation of the *Children and Young Persons Act*, 1969, because of this restriction on their powers.

11. Juvenile crime and the background of social services. Such provisions in the social services as the granting of family allowances, social security, public health and education, together with the local authority welfare services, might, it would seem, stave off the mental ills and social unhappiness caused by lack of material resources, poor health and lack of educational opportunities. The recognition of the importance of the family environment is evident in the proposals noted in **9** (*b*) and (*c*) above. The *Seebohm Committee* was set up in January 1966 to consider the organisation of responsibilities of the local authority social services in England and Wales and to consider what changes were desirable to secure an effective family service. Its findings were published in July 1968, under the title of *Local Authority and Allied Personal Social Services*.

(*a*) Its main recommendation was that all major local authorities should have a *social service department* administering all the various social welfare services for those living as part of a *family*, *e.g.* for the children, the elderly, the handicapped and the mentally ill.

(*b*) One *central government department* should be responsible for the new social service departments and for the overall planning and research in the social services. The *Local Authority Social Services Act*, 1970, enjoined the creation of such social service departments.

Social services provide only the framework of social security for the members of a community. The distinguishing characteristic of a true civilisation is the *moral integrity* of its society. For the survival of a society as a whole, old-fashioned ideas of "right" and "wrong" and adherence to moral standards will be more valuable than sociological explanations, and determination to refuse to depart from those standards of more practical value than excuses for their repudiation.

PROGRESS TEST 12

1. What is a crime?   (**1**)
2. Distinguish between indictable and non-indictable offences. (**1**)
3. Discuss four theories of punishment.   (**2**)
4. What are the major facts relating to tendencies in crime in Britain?   (**4**)
5. What are the broad features of juvenile crime?   (**5**)
6. What legislation before the 1930s was concerned with juvenile offenders?   (**6**)
7. State the main recommendations of the Ingleby Report, 1960. Which of these recommendations were accepted by the Government of the day?   (**7**)
8. What did the *Children and Young Persons Act*, 1963, seek to provide?   (**7, 9**)
9. What have been the categories of penalties imposed on juvenile offenders?   (**8**)
10. Which White Papers recently published have been concerned with the problem of juvenile offenders?   State their main recommendations.   (**9**)
11. What changes in the law relating to juvenile offenders have been made by the *Children and Young Persons Act*, 1969?   (**10**)
12. State the major recommendations of the Seebohm Committee Report, 1968.   (**11**)
13. "To deal with crime, social services, like patriotism, are not enough."   Comment.   (**11**)

CHAPTER XIII

THE ECONOMIC BACKGROUND

ECONOMICS AND EMPLOYMENT

1. Economics as a social science. The great economist Alfred Marshall defined economics, or political economy as it was called in the nineteenth century, as "the study of man's actions in the ordinary business of life; it inquires how he gets his income and how he spends it. Thus it is on the one side a study of wealth, and on the other, more important side, a part of the study of man" (*Principles of Economics* (Macmillan, 1890)). The word comes from the Greek and refers to house-keeping; as a social science it enquires into the ways in which communities manage their material affairs and make a living. The efforts of a community to make a living are the sum of the efforts of the individuals composing the community; the individual person has an ascribed or achieved economic status in his community, and plays such a role as will enable him to maintain or improve his status (*see* VII, 12). The urge towards a career, with its financial advantage or, broadly, the urge to "power," was one of the urges stated by the psychologist Alfred Adler to be fundamental to the individual (the others were the sex urge, the term being interpreted widely to include family life, and the urge towards a social life).

2. The transition from school to work. Most people have to go out into the world and make a living, working for hire or reward for another individual or for a corporation. The transformation of a schoolchild into a worker is similar in its impact on the human personality to the transformation from childhood to maturity, for having to make a living hastens maturity.

(*a*) The process may be painful for some temperaments, and may be deferred by the adoption of a university course which protects the student who may not be of an academic or university type.

(b) A continuation of the scholastic and sheltered atmosphere may merely be a protraction of an adolescent phase which must be experienced if the individual is to achieve a degree of maturity. Student revolts and demonstrations are often a manifestation of the pain felt by a young person coming to terms with the economic environment (see IV, 17 (d) and X, 8 (a)).

Where work can be transformed to a large extent from labour into "non-work," because of the interest attached to the occupation and the satisfaction to be obtained by doing something which has not only a personal but also a social value, e.g. medicine, the law, the arts and science, preparation for it can be begun early and sustained through life. Though at times working can be monotonous and even unpleasant, generally speaking the consequences of the division of labour and the remoteness of the individual from his final product, which often happens in a modern industrialised community, need not be too great a bar to personal satisfaction.

3. Apprenticeship. In the industrial environment the introduction into a skilled trade has formerly been by way of apprenticeship. It seems that in recent years the apprenticeship basis of training has not been maintained (see Gertrude Williams, *Recruitment to Skilled Trades* (Routledge and Kegan Paul, 1957)). A process of "picking it up" has superseded intensive training on the job. An investigation by Kate Liepmann, *Apprenticeship* (Routledge and Kegan Paul, 1960), indicates that apprenticeship has been transformed into a trade union weapon to serve as an argument for demarcation and to claim differentials in wages.

4. The Industrial Training Act, 1964. A modern equivalent of apprenticeship has been introduced by the *Industrial Training Act*, 1964 (*see also* X, 7 (d)). The Act provided for the establishment of Industrial Training Boards to promote and supervise standards of training throughout industry. A compulsory levy system has been combined with the payment of grants to those employers providing approved training activities for employees in firms' workshops, in Industrial

Training Board Centres and in technical colleges. A condition of a grant is that employees are released to attend an appropriate course of further education.

(a) The system has been extended to cover workers in non-manual employment, e.g. local government officers, where it has been integrated with the National Certificate system, in which part-time day-release preparation is made for examinations relating to the professional work of employees.

(b) The idea has been received with much opposition from farmers.

5. Further and higher education. Statistics relating to further and higher education are given in X, 7 (e).

(a) The technological universities were created in response to the demands of a technological age in which science has been applied to economic ends—the attainment of a higher material standard of living.

(b) Political interests are also involved, political leaders being concerned with problems of defence and prestige, e.g. space developments.

(c) University students are more concerned with the preparation for making a living than formerly, when knowledge was pursued for its own sake, or as part of the fulfilment of an ascribed status and role in the community (see VII, **12**).

(d) "Sandwich" courses in technical colleges—six months in industry and six months' full-time education—enable students to combine academic studies with industrial experience.

THE CHANGING ECONOMIC SCENE

6. The historical background. Max Weber (see III, **11** (d)) believed that the Puritan sects of the sixteenth century were responsible for the emergence of the religious sanctions and approvals attached to hard work and thrift, regarded as "cultural imperatives" (see R. H. Tawney, *Religion and the Rise of Capitalism* (John Murray, 1926, Penguin Books, 1966)).

(a) The conviction that material success was the reward of a life of hard work and thrift and sobriety whereas poverty was the result of lack of religious and moral fibre inspired the penal spirit of the nineteenth century that found its expression in the institution of workhouses and in the *Poor Law Amendment Act* of 1834. A principle of the Act was "less eligibility"—the giving of relief to the poor in such a way and on such a scale as would keep the position of the person below that of the lowest-paid worker. To quote Benjamin Disraeli, newly elected to the House of Commons, "in England poverty is a crime."

(b) It was only with the Minority Report of the Poor Law Commission of 1908 and the promulgation of Fabian ideas, like those of Mrs Beatrice Webb and the Socialist reformers, that it became accepted by the middle classes that poverty was not the result of divine visitation for sin but was the result of low wages due to family obligations, bad health, sheer misfortune and lack of skill.

(c) The Liberal reforms of the early twentieth century, including the *National Insurance Act*, 1911, extended by the post-war legislation and the beginnings of the Welfare State, have built up the social security provisions, including the National Health and welfare facilities, and the educational and training services which characterise the economic and social background in Britain.

(d) There is still inequality of wealth in the country: five per cent of the population own 95 per cent of the wealth, estimated at some £138,000 million. If it were divided equally, each married couple in Britain would be £9 a week better off. But it is very doubtful as to how far such a distribution would be useful, or even equitable.

7. The background of the planned economy. The experience of the unemployment of the 1930s, the confusions of the post-war era, the trade union consolidation of the post-war years and the consciousness of the increasing power of the worker, who knows that by concerted action he can destroy the industrial fabric of society (even if he destroys himself in the process) have interacted with one another and have influenced political action. In 1944 Lord Beveridge's *Full Employment in a Free Society* (Allen and Unwin) set out the broad lines on which the British economy must be planned if mass unemployment were not to be repeated. Governments, conscious of the controls and discipline necessary for the achievement of this aim, have been reluctantly compelled to move along these lines, so that there is no longer the policy of *laissez-faire* but of continuing change and adjustment, which moves towards economic as well as a social security. The worker has to pay the price of security and full employment by government or trade union control and direction.

8. Government control.

(*a*) In the 1930s, "Special Areas," later to be called "Development Areas," were given assistance by the Government towards rehabilitation. The *Local Employment Acts* of 1960 and 1963 gave the Board of Trade powers to provide employment in designated "Development Districts" which were replaced in 1966 by "Development Areas" in Scotland, Wales and the North of England.

(*b*) In November 1963, the Conservative Government published White Papers on the proposed development of North-East England and Central Scotland.

(*c*) A *National Economic Development Council* ("Neddy") was set up by the Conservatives in 1961 to advise the Government on the conditions of economic growth.

(*d*) When the Labour Government came to power in 1964 it started a programme of economic planning.

(*i*) The *Department of Economic Affairs* was set up in 1964, responsible for the long-term aspects of economic planning. It was wound up in 1969.

(*ii*) It worked with the National Economic Development Council and with the Economic Development Committees (the "Little Neddies"), reporting on the problems of efficiency of individual industries.

(*e*) *Regional Planning Boards* and *Councils* were set up for the eight *Economic Planning Regions* established in England between 1964 and 1966 for the particular study of the economic problems of these regions, with reference to population pressure, jobs and housing.

(*f*) The *Hunt Committee* reported on the intermediate areas (the "grey" areas) in April 1969.

(*g*) By various methods the government has endeavoured to achieve a balance of industry throughout the country, to avoid pockets of unemployment in some places and a surplus of jobs in another. A planned economy must exert a *pressure* on workers as well as on employers, who have been further influenced by a selective employment tax in that the employment of "service" workers was discouraged and the employment of directly productive workers encouraged. The workers displayed little enthusiasm for the "National Plan" of 1965.

9. Work categories. A glance at the statistics for the working population given in the *Monthly Digest of Statistics* (H.M.S.O.) or the *Gazette* of the Department of Employment will show the numbers engaged in the various occupations.

(a) The majority of workers are employed in the *private sector*, *i.e.* are employed by a private-enterprise organisation.

(b) About 8 per cent of the total labour force are employed by the *nationalised industries*, *i.e.* the Post Office, the National Coal Board, the British Gas Corporation and its regional organisations, the Electricity Boards, the airways corporations and the British Airports Authority, and the nationalised transport undertakings.

(c) The range of work in the modern economic scene is wide, from the professional worker in the Civil Service, the public corporations, insurance, and banking and the executive ranks of private enterprise, to storekeepers and cleaners. The vast majority of workers (about 30 per cent) are in the skilled manual-worker class followed by the semi-skilled (about 15 per cent) and the junior non-manual (about 12 per cent) and the unskilled (about $8\frac{1}{2}$ per cent). Apart from the self-employed and the managers of small establishments, the great majority of workers are in subordinate positions and, if they are not skilled workers, find their way of making a living to a great extent irksome.

(d) Fifty per cent of the men in the factories and offices in Britain have earned *less* than £24 a week, one in every twelve less than £15, and twenty-five per cent of the women less than £10 a week. Farmworkers have been the lowest-paid men (an average of about £11·70 per week) and waitresses the lowest-paid women (an average of £6).

10. Problems of the work situation. The work situation of most people seems to be one in which the features of Rostow's "high mass production stage" have been realised (*see* **IV, 10** (*e*)). One feature of this age has been the *alienation* of the

worker from his work, and in many cases boredom and
hatred of the machine-like existence of some assembly-line
workers, as L. Libitz observed in a study of manual workers in
the U.S.A.

(a) The use of "industrial psychology" techniques, per-
sonnel management and joint consultation devices can only
be palliative. The problem is one of the *raison d'être* of
industry—what is industry for, how can material wealth be
produced with the least wear and tear on the human
personality and how is the wealth to be distributed when it
has been produced? These are the major problems of the
economic background to the social structure.

(b) The individual person in a modern industrialised
society has to solve his own problems of life, work and
leisure, and failure to come to terms with his work will
produce *conflict*, a conflict which will be produced on a
larger scale in society (*see* IV, **16** and **17**).

NOTE: For a discussion of British working-class life, with special
reference to publications and entertainments, see Richard
Hoggart, *The Uses of Literacy* (Chatto and Windus, 1957).

PROGRESS TEST 13

1. What is economics as a social science? **(1)**
2. What is the place of the individual in the economic life of
the community in which he lives? **(1)**
3. What are the difficulties faced by the individual in the
transition from school to work? **(2)**
4. Is apprenticeship still of importance as an introduction to a
skilled trade? **(3)**
5. State the major provisions of the *Industrial Training Act,
1964*. **(4)**
6. What are the methods of obtaining technological education
and training in further and higher education? **(5)**
7. How has the social background of work and security changed
since the nineteenth century? **(6)**
8. Review the background of the economic planning by the
Government since the 1930s. **(7, 8)**
9. What is the general pattern of the work categories in
Britain? **(9)**
10. What are the main problems of the work situation today?
(10)

CHAPTER XIV

THE POLITICAL ENVIRONMENT

THE POLITICAL SYSTEM

1. The necessity for government. Except among the most primitive of peoples there is always some sort of political organisation (even if it is only an occasional gathering of chiefs or elders), which lays down rules for ordering the life of the community and interpreting its customs.

NOTE: Theories of the functions of the state have been considered in II.

2. The problem of modern politics. In modern industrial societies the problem of politics resolves itself into the question of how the necessity for government, with its complications of welfare services and economic planning (discussed in XIII), can be *reconciled* with the necessity for preserving the liberties of the individual.

3. The British Constitution. This HANDBOOK is not the place for a discussion of forms of political machinery and organs of government, which have received, are receiving and will receive voluminous treatment in hundreds of works. The sociologist, thinking as a political sociologist about political systems and, in particular, the political system of his own country, must have some sort of criteria by which he can estimate the efficacy of a political system in terms of the social structure. The clue to the problem is given by the term *system*: the political system in Britain is much more a *system* than the economic complex, with its wide range of *laissez-faire* and free-enterprise activity. The British Constitution is a system of rules, some "legal," some conventional, some written, some unwritten—as is the *common law*—by which the relationships between the governed and the government are regulated.

The Constitution may be changed by the ordinary processes of legislation: it is *flexible*, unlike the Constitution of the United States of America, which can be changed only by a special process. However, how it may be changed depends upon the pressures exerted by respective political parties.

4. The British party system. In Britain there are two major political parties, Labour and Conservative, with the Liberal Party a minor but more cohesive and stable party than any of the other small groups formed from time to time.

(*a*) The parties are *associations*, not institutions (*see* VII, **3** and **6**). They are pressure groups, organised to serve the interests of their members, and cannot speak for the nation, as both the major parties suggest they do. The Labour Party, especially, as a mixture of working-class and trade-union supporters on the one hand (though not all trade unionists support the Labour Party), and doctrinaire Socialists on the other, is inclined to regard the Constitution with considerably less reverence than the Conservatives.

(*b*) Nowadays, the terms "left" and "right" are more descriptive than "Labour" or "Socialist," or "Conservative" or "Tory" (the latter term containing an element of abuse), since many of the supporters of the Labour Party merely desire a more equitable distribution of wealth and more control of the economy by the state rather than outright Socialist control, and many supporters of the Conservative Party favour cautious progress towards these ends. People can be "left of centre" or "right of centre."

(*c*) Because of the *anomalies* of the single-member, single-vote system, which does not allocate seats in the Commons in accordance with the number of votes cast, it may often happen that a party can obtain a *majority of seats* in the Commons whilst a *majority of votes* has been cast against it, *e.g.* the 1970 General Election (*see* **8** below).

(*d*) In such circumstances, though a successful party can claim that it has a "mandate" to govern, it cannot claim that it has a mandate to put party policy into practice when it is opposed by both the Commons and the public, for although the use of a party majority may ensure the legal acceptance of a policy, that policy may well be against the wishes of the majority of the people.

5. The organisation of the parties. A party is organised both inside and outside Parliament.

(a) Inside Parliament is the *Parliamentary party*, consisting of Members of Parliament led by a Leader and disciplined by the Whips.

(i) The Leader of the party with a majority of seats becomes the *Prime Minister*, and he forms a *Cabinet* and a *Government*. The rank-and-file Members are known as "back-benchers."

(ii) The Leader of the party with the next largest number of supporters becomes the *Leader of the Opposition*—"Her Majesty's Opposition"—who has a *constitutional* position, marked by his being paid a salary. He forms a "Shadow Cabinet" ready to fulfil the major function of the Opposition, which is to take over the government of the country should the existing Government go out of office.

(b) Outside Parliament is the national party organisation, with headquarters in a Central Office and with local party organisations in the constituencies; it is responsible for choosing candidates for Parliamentary seats, producing party propaganda and conducting election campaigns.

6. The organisation of the Conservative Party. The full title of the Conservative Party is the "National Union of Conservative and Unionist Associations."

(a) The *Central Council*, consisting of the Parliamentary party, adopted candidates and representatives from the constituency associations, is in theory the executive organ, but in practice the Central Office organises the political activities.

(b) The *Annual Conference*, attended by all the members of the Central Council, with the election agents and representatives from each constituency, is a gathering for the general expression of Conservative opinion.

(c) Until 1965, the *Leader* of the Party was chosen by consultation between the Conservative Members of both Houses of Parliament, the prospective Party candidates and the executive committee of the National Union of Conservative and Unionist Associations. In February 1965, a new procedure was adopted whereby the Leader is now elected by *ballot* of the Parliamentary Members, their

choice being formally subject to the final approval of
M.P.s, prospective candidates, peers and the National Union
Executive.

(*d*) The Leader directs the Conservative Central Office
and appoints the Chairman of the Party. He is in a more
powerful position in relation to his party than the Labour
Leader because the Conservative Party is more homo-
geneous than the Labour Party and its political aims are
more capable of simple expression, though the old Tory
creed "I hold what I have" is now overlaid with democratic
ideas. It is not proposed, however, to discuss the political
philosophy of "democracy" in this HANDBOOK.

7. The Liberal Party. It may be said that "left" Con-
servatism approaches the Liberalism of the Liberal Party.
This party has a traditional policy of free trade and its
"intellectual" members favour an intellectual Socialism,
expressing itself in ideas of profit-sharing in industry, labour
participation in management, reform of the electoral system
towards proportional representation (the number of seats
according to votes, which would be of great advantage to the
Liberals) and devolution (regional Parliaments). It is the
idealistic party, and its ideas and programme are considered
by supporters of the other Parties to be impracticable.

8. The Labour Party organisation. Powerful factors in the
Labour organisation are the trade union members and the
co-operative societies. Of more than 9 million members
of trade unions affiliated to the Party, 5 million pay a
political levy. (At the 1970 General Election 12·1 million people
voted for the Labour Party, 13·1 million for the Conservative
Party, 2·1 million for the Liberals, 38,431 for the Communists
and about 865,000 for other candidates.) The general features
of the Labour Party organisation are as follows:

(*a*) Constituencies are divided into wards, and wards are
grouped into Regional Councils.

(*b*) The headquarters are at Transport House, the General
Secretary of which is appointed by the National Executive
Committee.

(*c*) The twenty-eight members of the National Executive
Committee are elected by the Annual Labour Conference,

composed of delegates of trade unions, Socialist societies, divisional Labour Parties and other affiliated organisations, including the local branches of co-operative societies.

(*d*) The Leader and Deputy Leader of the Party are *ex-officio* members of the National Executive Committee.

(*e*) The Leader of the Party is elected *annually* by the Parliamentary Labour Party (though it is customary to re-elect him).

(*f*) The existence of a National Executive is an embarrassment to a Labour Government, for the National Executive Committee draws up a programme which is debated at the Annual Party Conference—and is essentially a *Labour* programme. A government of whatever party has a responsibility to the *nation as a whole*, whereas the Labour Conference is responsible only to itself. *Conflict* may arise, and has arisen, between the National Executive and the Parliamentary leaders, whether in the Government or in the Opposition, over policy. The more extreme members of a National Executive Committee may propose a Socialist policy which a responsible Labour Government may be reluctant to adopt.

(*g*) A matter of constitutional importance is the position of the House of Lords: Labour policy tends towards the reduction of its delaying power, and extremists would like to abolish it altogether.

NOTE: The details of the Constitution and the government of the nation cannot be dealt with in this **HANDBOOK**. They are discussed in the author's *British Constitution and Government* (The **HANDBOOK** Series, Macdonald and Evans, Second Edition, 1973).

PRESSURE GROUPS AND PUBLIC OPINION

9. Pressure groups. Members of Parliament are subject to "pressure groups" which *lobby* M.P.s and try to urge courses of action upon them, *e.g.* the National Federation of Women's Institutes.

(*a*) The political parties and party organisations are themselves *pressure groups*. Though they employ sanctions in disciplining their members, they are not institutions (*see*

4 (*a*) they have to work within the framework of the Constitution if social stability is to be maintained.

(*b*) *Trade unions* are also large pressure groups.

(*i*) The unions are separate bodies, though for common action they may form *confederations*.

(*ii*) Members are attached to *branches*, which are grouped into *districts*, with district or area councils or committees, represented on *national committees*.

(*iii*) The trade unions provide their own elected or appointed *full-time officials*, called variously District Organisers, Divisional Officers, etc.

(*iv*) The representative on the shop floor is a voluntary worker called a *shop steward* or shop representative.

(*v*) The *Trades Union Congress* is the annual "Parliament" of trade union members, constituted by the affiliation of trade unions. It has no executive authority over the unions: in 1969 the T.U.C. persuaded the Labour Government that it could deal with unauthorised strikes by its own authority (being unwilling to agree to the Government's proposals for legislation), but it failed to do so.

(*c*) On the employers' side the *Confederation of British Industry* is a federation resulting from the merging of the three largest federations in 1963.

(*d*) One pressure group with an influence quite disproportionate to its numbers is the Lord's Day Observance Society, operating with funds largely derived from wills and donations.

(*e*) The "whipping system" protects Members of Parliament from insistent pressure groups, since a Member can plead the necessity of having to conform to *force majeure* (party pressure).

10. Elites. An élite is a class of persons who are distinguished in a particular sphere and exercise authority, moral or practical, in that sphere, *e.g.* in the arts, in the sciences, in politics (see T. B. Bottomore, *Elites in Society* (Watts, 1964) for a summary of theories of the élites).

(*a*) Elites are of considerable importance in the social structure, since they are the leaders in their particular spheres and help to form the *standards* by which social progress in a particular field is judged.

(*b*) Elites may not be recognised as such in their time—

the story of posthumous fame is a common one—but their *influence* is ultimately of more weight than the ephemeral success, say, of pop singers.

(c) An élite may exercise power "behind the scenes"; *e.g.* the administrative class of the Civil Service, whose knowledge and expertise in administrative matters have had a considerable influence on politicians.

(d) There is no longer a "ruling class" of the traditional type in Britain, consisting of a specially educated and wealthy property-owning class, an élite consisting of an "Establishment" and providing a governing class.

(i) In a democracy, power is diffused, and rests ultimately in the electorate.   In Switzerland, which is a confederation of republics, the cantons, no politician is allowed to achieve a position of undue political power.

(ii) In the U.S.S.R., however, there is an élite, the Communist Party, which is a comparatively small body, proportional to the population.   Its members have been politically trained from youth, and are distinguished by the rigidity of their ideology and their knowledge of Marxist principles and creeds.   This élite is the ruling class (*see* V, 2 (b)).

11. Public opinion.   "Public opinion" is a somewhat vague expression; in a democracy it means the free expression of opinion by individuals and groups, in the press, on platforms and in the communication media generally, so that there emerges a body of opinion of which politicians take note.

(a) Often it is the *articulate and definite expression* of a general body of views which is held only vaguely, indefinitely or inarticulately by a large body of people, *e.g.* the Common Market controversy in Britain.

(b) Very often it is the *reaction* of the general public to some government action.   Recent examples are as follows:

(i) The outcry in 1968 against the "two-tier" postal charges.

(ii) The dislike expressed in 1968 by a large section of the public about British Standard Time.

(iii) The concern in 1968 at the disbandment of the Argyll and Sutherland Regiment, expressed as a petition to the Commons with one million signatures.

Expressions of public opinion may not substantially change

the course of government policy; public opinion on government matters, like its taste for entertainers, is fickle and public memory is short, facts of which politicians are well aware. But *informed and organised opinion* with long-term public welfare in mind, *e.g.* that represented by the National Council for Civil Liberties, does generate and maintain a "climate of opinion" which politicians know they would be unwise to defy.

BUREAUCRACY AND POWER

12. The nature of a bureaucracy. A *bureaucracy* is a machinery of administration by which the executive power in a community (in Britain the "Crown," in effect the government) or in a large organisation, such as a nationalised industry, is carried into effect. In Britain, this administrative machinery of government is the Civil Service, following regulations and rules which have been laid down by the government and its administrative staff as being the most efficient, or at least the most adequate, way by which the wishes of the government, *e.g.* in the administration of the social services, can be carried out.

(*a*) It is this administrative machinery, consisting of civil servants, of employees of nationalised industries or large-scale undertakings, which is often referred to as the bureaucacy, or the "bureaucratic machine," although the expression "bureaucracy" is usually applied to central government and municipal administration, as is also the term "red tape." "Bureaucratic" is used most often with a derogatory implication, but it is frequently forgotten that government administration can function only when there is meticulous attention to detail and regulations.

(*b*) Max Weber (*see* III, 11 (*d*)) regarded a bureaucratic organisation, with a detailed division of labour and a hierarchy of officials, as necessary for the efficient running of the governmental affairs of a community.

13. The bureaucrat. Weber suggested that the rewards offered to a bureaucrat were not the normal and direct reward offered to other types of workers: the status in society and the satisfaction obtained from doing a job in the service of one's country constituted rewards apart from the financial ones.

(a) There appears to be a great deal of truth in this suggestion.   Certainly, in spite of the bureaucratic functions being called "dysfunctions" by Merton (*see* IV, **13** (*a*)),— *e.g.* the rigid adherence to rules, the narrowness of training, the isolation from the rest of the community, the stultification of the lives of the bureaucrats—the British Civil Service, though it has its faults and has its critics of its administration of such matters as the social services and the tax system, is still trusted and respected by the public, and is still generally regarded as being the best in the world.

(b) The introduction of *new techniques* of management, training and, following the Fulton Committee's recommendations in 1968, re-organisation, seem to invalidate those criticisms made in (*a*).

(c) Where there is no dynamic matching of circumstances with action, as in Italy at the present moment, bureaucracy and the bureaucrat are not held in such high regard; the post of Minister for Bureaucratic Reform in the Italian Cabinet has existed for years without producing anything to lessen the frustration of the people.

(d) Where there is a "spoils" system, as in the U.S.A., where many jobs are re-allocated on a change of government, corruption must occur.

(e) A study by Nigel Walker, *Morale in the Civil Service* (Edinburgh University Press, 1961), showed a satisfaction amongst British civil servants.   Mr Walker found no correlation between efficiency and satisfaction in the job; there were fewer persons dissatisfied with their low-grade jobs than there were in the highest grade.   There seemed to be some correlation with efficiency and age, the highest efficiency being attributed to the thirty to thirty-nine age group—a result not inconsistent with what would be expected in most jobs.

14. The "conflict" theory of power.   According to some sociologists, social changes occur as the result of the shifting balance of power between groups in conflict.   It may equally be argued that conflicts occur as the result of social changes.

(a) The conflicts between the *trade unions and employers*

have occurred as social changes produced trade unions and new-style employers.

(b) The *class antagonisms* that exist do so because social changes have resulted in the emergence of new classes and the need for adjustments in the social structure (*see* IX).

(c) In *political life*, conflicts have occurred because of the clash of interests brought about by changes in the social and economic structure. Karl Marx (*see* II, **18** (*g*)) attributed the whole history of social change to a class struggle between the owners of property and the property-less proletariat exploited by the capitalists. Alternatively, one could suggest that such a struggle would occur as the *result* of social changes; it could certainly be argued that the conflict between the U.S.S.R. and Czechoslovakia in 1968 arose from the social changes which were taking place in Czechoslovakia and which threatened the stability of the Soviet system itself.

NOTE: *See* IV, **17** for conflict in society.

15. The dangers of bureaucracy. The dangers of bureaucracy are the same as those connected with all large organisations which can exercise power over the governed, subject to legal or military sanctions: the abuse of that power in the interests of the organisers, the multiplication of jobs, statuses and roles (*see* VII, **12**) for their own sake and, in the ultimate stage, the subordination of the individual to the claims of the administrative machine and the persons directing the machine. The price of liberty is eternal vigilance.

(a) The domination of the Nazi Party in Germany—a minority party—was obtained by ruthlessness and efficient organisation, a cause and effect demonstrated by Hitler theoretically in *Mein Kampf* and practically by his own actions.

(b) The efficiency and ruthlessness of the Communist Party in the U.S.S.R. have also been demonstrated.

(c) Were it not for the efficiency of the organisation of states, there would be no "global" or "continental" wars, for the ordinary person in all states does not want them. Organisation marshals the forces of propaganda, makes easy the formation of a military machine and smothers resistance to the idea of war.

(*d*) Equally, the success of such bodies as UNO, UNESCO and the Red Cross depends upon the organisation of technical ability, such as that possessed by economists and scientists, in an efficient and bureaucratic way.   Since their aims are beneficent, an excess of bureaucracy does comparatively little harm.

PROGRESS TEST 14

1. Why is government necessary?   (**1, 2**)

2. Is there a political *system* in Britain?   (**3**)

3. Why are the British political parties *associations* and not *institutions?*   (**4, 9**)

4. How are the political parties organised?   (**4, 5**)

5. How is the Conservative Party organised?   (**6**)

6. What are the characteristics of the Liberal Party?   (**7**)

7. How is the Labour Party organised?   (**8**)

8. What are pressure groups?   Give examples.   (**9**)

9. How are the trade unions organised?   (**9**)

10. What is an élite?   Give examples of élites.   How is an élite distinguished from a ruling class?   (**10**)

11. What is "public opinion"?   How is it expressed?   (**11**)

12. What is a bureaucracy?   (**12**)

13. What faults have been attributed specially to bureaucrats? Are they justified?   (**13**)

14. What is the "conflict" theory of power?   (**14**)

15. What are the dangers of bureaucracy?   (**15**)

CHAPTER XV

POPULATION

POPULATION EXPANSION

1. Population problems. One of the major problems confronting an expanding industrialised society is the pressure of population on its resources. An increase of resources and improvements in the standard of living would appear to be more successful solutions than the spread of contraceptive devices, but only in the short term. There is a tendency to marry early (*see* VIII, **14**), and the ability to get jobs seems to be linked with setting up a home and starting a family. With conurbations, with industrial areas spreading and with more firms catering for more markets, there could arise a vicious circle of population growth, urbanisation and the turning of a pleasant country into vast industrial area—a consummation most devoutly not to be wished.

2. The "optimum" population. This expression has been used to refer to that population which under existing technical conditions will result in the greatest production per head. This term considers the problem from a purely economic point of view, and not even from the point of view of welfare economics. In a large, empty country the "optimum" population might require a woman to have twenty children, a state of affairs beneficial neither for the woman, the family, nor, in the long run, the community.

3. Malthusianism. The miseries of the poor in France before the Revolution and the expansion of population in Britain during the course of the Industrial Revolution were phenomena which engaged the attention of Thomas Malthus, a clergyman, whose *Essay on the Principles of Population as it Affects the Future Improvement of Society* was first published in 1798, a revised version appearing in 1803. In 1700 the population of Britain was about 6½ million, and between 1760 and 1820 it increased to over 12 million.   Between 1801 and 1901 it multiplied three-and-a-half times.   In 1801 (the date of the first census) the population of England and Wales was 8,893,000; in 1901 it was 32,528,000; in 1951 it was 43,758,000; in 1966, 48,075,000; and in 1970, 48,988,000 (estimated).

(a) Malthus's *thesis* was that population tended to outstrip the food supply.   Disastrous over-population could only be prevented by two kinds of checks:

   (i) *Positive:* war, disease, famine and vice.
   (ii) *Preventive:* prudence and self-control.

(b) Malthus has been criticised for his *pessimism* and his failure to take account of the technological developments arising from the application of science to industry and agriculture, making larger populations possible, and a rise in the standard of living.   It is doubtful whether he would have regarded modern contraceptive devices as vice or prudence.

(c) Nevertheless, though improvements in technology and control over the material environment can postpone a crisis, they cannot eliminate it completely: obviously, an unchecked rise in population can be disastrous.   "Standing room only" is not a pleasant prospect, and burrowing under the ground or colonising the moon has its limits, if only in attractiveness.

4. World population.   Malthus's analysis was undoubtedly correct as far as the less developed countries of the world are concerned.

(a) The world's population of about 3,800 million has been increasing at the rate of about 1·7 per cent per annum. It is expected to have doubled by the year 2000.   The increase is expected to occur mainly in the less developed countries, where about half the world's population already lives.

(b) In the eleven years previous to 1961 the world's population increased by 560 million: 60 per cent of this increase live in *Asia*, where the population is expected to be about 3,870 million by the year 2000.

(c) Thirty per cent of the world's population live in the *richer* countries—North America, Europe, Russia, Australia,

New Zealand and Japan. An estimate by the United Nations Organisation is that if present tendencies continue about 90 per cent of the world's wealth will be owned by less than one-quarter of the world's population.

(d) The *implications* of these facts may be serious, but there is no need to assume that there will be a nuclear holocaust. *Aid*, including technical aid, to the less developed countries by the more industrialised countries, is one of the many strands which will shape the fabric of the future.

5. Population in the United Kingdom. It has been a characteristic of forecasts of the population of Britain that they have almost invariably been wrong: the variables, economic, political, social and psychological, have been too many to take adequately into account. Assumptions of future birth rates, in particular, are subject to a wide margin of error, although assumptions of death rates and migration for the near future are less likely to cause errors in "projections" (a term less liable to criticism than "forecasts").

(a) In the year 1951 the population of the U.K. was 50·6 million; in 1967, it was 55·2 million. According to projections issued in November 1971, by the Office of Population Censuses and Surveys, the population of Britain in 2001 will be 66·5 million; an increase of $\frac{1}{2}$ per cent each year until 1980 and a slightly higher rate after that.

(b) In 1960, out of a total population of 52·5 million, 34·2 million were of *working age*, *i.e.* between fifteen and sixty-four for men, and fifteen and fifty-nine for women.

(c) People of normal working age have *declined* as a proportion of the population since 1951, and the projections indicate that they will form an even *smaller* proportion in 1981. However, the proportion will *increase* between 1981 and 2001.

(d) Between 1967 and 1981 the number of workers (35·4 million in 1967) will *increase* by about 5 per cent, while the number of people over the present retiring age will increase by 14 per cent. Between 1981 and 2001, while the workers will increase by about 20 per cent, the retired people will slightly decrease.

(e) During both periods, those under fifteen will have

increased by 16 per cent by 1981 and a further 28 per cent by 2001. The raising of the school-leaving age and the greater opportunities available in further and higher education will increase the numbers at school (*see* X, **5** and **7**).

(*f*) The casualties of the First World War have resulted in relatively low numbers of people over retiring age now, and the *low birth rates* between the wars have affected the number of both men and women over forty-five and will continue to affect this number. Malthus may well have been correct.

(*g*) By 2001, most people born between the wars will be retired. About 69 per cent of the population will be under forty-five, compared with 63 per cent in 1967.

(*h*) The implications of these statistics present very puzzling problems. Technology, the economic and political changes, the impact of scientific research in biology and health, and other factors of which at the moment we have only the vaguest ideas, will affect the population problems. "More gardening tools and fewer play-pens" is too naïve a comment on the probable changes in the structure of in-dustrial production. The technological advances made as a result of space-travel may have repercussions beyond their immediate impact on production techniques.

(*i*) In May 1971, a Select Committee of the House of Commons proposed that the Government should set up a permanent office to advise it on population trends. The Committee's report quoted estimates for Britain's popula-tion at June 1970, at 55,711,000 and a projection of 82.3 million for 2030 and considered the risks entailed to the environment and to the supply of food and jobs. The Committee stated that the pressure of population growth could make everyday life "intolerable."

THE EFFECTS OF INCREASING POPULATION

6. The Royal Commission on Population, 1944. The belief that the population was about to decline and concern at the nature of the trends at the time inspired the appointment of a Royal Commission on Population which reported in 1949. It was this belief which influenced Lord Beveridge to suggest the provision of family allowances. The Report of the Economic

Committee of the Commission, 1950, suggested four main advantages of an increasing population. They are as follows:

(*a*) There is an *increase* in the scale of production, and the *stimulation* of technical improvements.

(*i*) These events will probably take place.

(*ii*) However, the worst effects of Rostow's final stage of industrialisation (*see* IV, **10** (*e*)) may also occur.

(*b*) With a high birth rate, there is a low *average age of population*.

(*i*) There is no virtue in "youth" as such.

(*ii*) Observation in factories shows that older people are steadier and more reliable than the young and have greater experience. Greater maturity is no longer necessarily accompanied by senility.

(*c*) There is a greater *flexibility* in the economic system, so that mass unemployment is avoided.

(*i*) Where there is too great a specialisation, unemployment will occur in response to world conditions. "King Cotton" was dethroned in Lancashire as the result of a lack of flexibility in the cotton industry and Japanese competition. In 1952 part of South-east Lancashire was scheduled as a "Development Area" (*see* XIII, **8** (*a*)).

(*ii*) *Automation* has resulted in considerable unemployment in the United States. Automation has the opposite effect to that of division of labour—there are fewer jobs for more people.

(*d*) There is a *strengthening* of the international position and therefore the economic position of the nation.

(*i*) However, in a nuclear war a large population densely concentrated in industrial areas would be at a great disadvantage.

(*ii*) Sweden's population is about one-sixth that of Britain, and the German Federal Republic's strength at the moment does not depend on its numbers (about 60 million).

The *disadvantages* cited by the Committee referred to the decrease in the amount of land per head, and the diversion of resources, which would have gone to raising the standard of living, to the provision of capital equipment. The former would apply only where there was a lack of progress in farming or to a tendency towards a very dense population, and the latter seems a somewhat distorted argument—there must be provision for capital equipment or there would not be any consumption goods.

7. The Phillips Committee Report, 1954. The possibility of an increase in the proportion of older people being supported by the working population has seemed to present terrors to some investigators. In the Phillips Report, *The Report of the Committee on the Economic and Financial Problems of the Provision for Old Age* (Cmnd. 9333, H.M.S.O., 1954), it was suggested that the age at which the National Insurance retirement pension could be claimed at standard rate should be raised. Two comments can be made on this suggestion:

(*a*) The older people *have made their contribution* to national resources; there would not be any national resources if it had not been for the efforts of the older people.

(*b*) Possible productivity is such now that the "cost" of providing for the old could be a very minor problem. A correct planning of economic resources, an absence of "wildcat" strikes, demarcation disputes and restrictive practices (on both sides of industry) would result in there being more than enough for everybody (*see* XIII and IV, **10** (*e*)).

8. The dangers of expansion. The Royal Commission on Population mentioned the distinction between quantity and quality: it stated that the average size of family of the unskilled worker was twice as large as that of the professional and administrative workers. One might question what is meant by "quality"; it is relevant to point out that serious facts may be concealed within the statement of statistics. The proportion of mentally defective people in England and Wales increased by 21 per cent between 1891 and 1901, compared with an increase of only 3 per cent in the previous decade. Prudence and self-control are not qualities found in those least likely to found good families. The point raises such matters as compulsory sterilisation, enforced contraception and genetic control: highly controversial subjects.

9. Population distribution since the Industrial Revolution. The industrial expansion since the late eighteenth century affected not only the number but also the distribution of the population.

(a) In 1700 less than *one-fifth* of the population lived in towns, but by 1850 *half* the population was living in towns.

(b) *Increases and concentrations* of population occurred in the London area, in the cotton-manufacturing areas, in the coalfields and in the industrial areas of the Midlands.

(c) *Economic dislocations and depressions* therefore affected the concentration when techniques and market conditions changed. The old, established, heavy industries declined and the North and East became derelict, whilst the population of London and the home counties increased and light industry, with new resources of electrical power, attracted markets and workers. These dislocations necessitated the remedies described in XIII, 7 and 8. They include the intensified efforts on the part of the Government to plan population as well as economic patterns.

IMMIGRATION

10. Commonwealth immigration. The prejudices and hostilities aroused by coloured immigrants inspired the Government to set up a Race Relations Board. A *Government survey* among immigrants took three years and was published in June 1969.

(a) The census, based on a 10-per-cent sample, distinguished between immigrants from the *old* Commonwealth countries (Australia, New Zealand and Canada) and the *new* Commonwealth countries (Kenya, Pakistan, etc.).

(b) In 1966 there were 853,000 "new" and 125,000 "old" immigrant citizens.

(c) Forty-three per cent of the "new" Commonwealth immigrants have settled in central London and 10 per cent in the West Midlands, with London's outer metropolitan area coming next in order.

(d) The immigrants owned and occupied 156,000 homes, whilst 30,000 were rented from local authorities or new town development corporations (*see* **13** (c) below).

(e) The average family had three or fewer children; only 11,500 out of 270,000 had five or more, although there was considerable over-crowding.

(f) The number of babies born into "new" Commonwealth families was 425,000.

(g) Eighty-five per cent of the "new" Commonwealth men were fully employed, and only three per cent were on state assistance.

(h) There was a good deal of inter-marriage: 17,000 Indians married British girls.

(i) The survey showed that most immigrants were anxious to merge into the British way of life.

11. Immigration problems. Migration did not play an important part in determining population in Britain until after the middle 1960s.   From 1871 to 1951 there was a net loss in population from migration from the United Kingdom. The trend was then reversed for England and Wales (not for Scotland and Northern Ireland).   From 1931 to 1961 there was a net gain for the United Kingdom of 477,000; for England and Wales, there was an increase of 1,145,000.   The situation took a serious turn in the view of some people when there appeared to be a large increase of *coloured immigrants*.   In the year 1968–9 there was a large influx of Asians from East Africa holding U.K. passports; over 7,000 arrived during the three months previous to February 1969, when a Bill was announced to control the immigration of people holding U.K. passports who had no substantial connection with the U.K. The Commonwealth Immigrants Bill received the Royal Assent on 1st March 1969.

The Rt. Hon. Enoch Powell, M.P., whose pronouncements on coloured immigration have provoked considerable controversy, stated at Bradford on 18th July 1969 that the Government had disclosed that the immigrant population had grown in the preceding two-and-a-half years from 1 million to 1,250,000.   He envisaged a coloured population of 3 million in 1985, unless the rate of natural increase diminished (this figure will represent five per cent of the population at that time). This coloured population would not be evenly distributed. The percentage of coloured births in nine of the twelve Inner London boroughs averaged 19 per cent, and Mr Powell suggested that many towns and boroughs (*e.g.* Birmingham, Bradford, Huddersfield) would have one quarter of their population coloured.   Concern had in fact been expressed at Wolverhampton, Mr Powell's constituency, and at Bradford, where the coloured ratio is one of the highest in Britain.

In July 1971, Mr. Powell claimed that the net immigration from the New Commonwealth between May 1970 and April 1971 was over 70,000—more than 10 per cent higher than in the earlier twelve months. But the Home Office stated that the settlement figures showed that the number of New Commonwealth immigrants had fallen from 33,942 (plus 6,249 largely East African U.K. citizens) in 1969 to 26,562 (plus 6,839 U.K. citizens) in 1970.

Controversy over the interpretation of statistics—and facts —has continued to the present time.

HOUSING AND TOWN PLANNING

12. **Housing.** The problem of increasing population has brought with it the question of providing homes. Though there has been this problem since the beginning of industrialisation, the acceptance of slums and the miseries of inadequate housing ceased with the turn of the century. Since then, there has been a battle to clear the slums, build homes and provide for the indigent by subsidies, rent control and rent rebate schemes, with the local authorities taking a major role.

(a) In 1965 the Labour Government published a White Paper *The Housing Programme 1965 to 1970* (Cmnd. 2838). It stated the following requirements:

(i) "*Needs existing now*: about 1 million houses to replace unfit houses already identified as *slums*; up to 2 million to *replace old houses* not yet slums but not worth improving; and about 700,000 to overcome *shortages* and provide a margin for mobility."

(ii) "*Needs arising annually*: 30,000 [houses] a year to replace the loss caused by *demolition*—road widening and other forms of redevelopment; and 150,000 a year to keep pace with *new households* being formed in the rising population."

It is evident that only by a system of applied priorities in building and labour employment, in relation to schools and industrial development, can this programme be fulfilled.

(*b*) The problem is complicated by such *disputes* as those concerning the subsidisation of council-house tenants by owner-occupiers, rent rebate schemes and rent control. The cry of "means test" is constantly raised when there is a suggestion that council-house rents should depend on tenants' incomes.

13. Town planning. Some attempts have been made by private enterprise towards the creation of "gracious living" in towns: Bourneville was established in 1879, Port Sunlight in 1888 and Letchworth Garden City in 1903. Ebenezer Howard's ideas on the ideals of town planning were published in *Garden Cities of Tomorrow* in 1898.

(*a*) In Britain *Town Planning Acts* have been passed since the early twentieth century to try to meet the problems of the proliferation of houses and streets and disorder.

(*b*) In the 1940s the reports of three committees were published, and as a result the Ministry of Town and Country Planning was created to implement these reports. The committees were as follows:

(*i*) The *Barlow* Committee on the Geographical Location of the Industrial Population (1940).

(*ii*) The *Scott* Committee on Land Utilisation in Rural Areas (1942).

(*iii*) The *Uthwatt* Committee on Compensation and Betterment (1942).

(*c*) The *New Towns Acts*, 1946–49, provided for the setting up of new towns by Development Corporations. When the task of establishing new towns had been fulfilled, the Corporations were to be dissolved and their powers transferred to a Commission for the New Towns. By 1967, twenty-two new towns had been created.

(*i*) Their problems have been the *shortage of amenities* such as meeting halls, cinemas and clubs, the *shortage of schools, high rents* for houses, and the *need for balancing industries*, since certain industries have predominated in various towns, *e.g.* steel in Corby.

(*ii*) The *lack of historical associations* and of a "folk spirit," usually accumulated through the years, are serious psychological drawbacks in a new town.

(*d*) The *Town Development Act*, 1952, provided for "receiving districts" to receive "overspill" populations from congested towns. The problem has been that of pouring new wine into old bottles (see Margaret Stacey, *Tradition and Change: A Study of Banbury* (Oxford University Press, 1960)).

(*e*) The activities of a *Land Commission*, established in 1967 to collect a "betterment" levy on the developed value of land, created considerable resentment and inflicted great hardship in individual cases—an outstanding example of the effects of untempered bureaucracy (*see* XIV, 12 and 13).

(*f*) *Regional* economic planning by Economic Planning Boards and Councils (*see* XIII, 8 (*e*)) has taken the problem of planning into the national field.

(*g*) In the meanwhile, the *proliferation* of motor-cars in an affluent society and the *congestion* created by undisciplined traffic on the roads have led to a situation examined in the Buchanan Report, *Traffic in Towns*, 1963.

PROGRESS TEST 15

1. What are the population problems facing an expanding, industrialised society? (1)

2. What is the "optimum" population? Has the conception any validity? (2)

3. What was Malthus's thesis? Was he correct? (3–5)

4. What are the major facts about world population? (4)

5. What are the major facts about the U.K. population? (5)

6. What were the main advantages and disadvantages of an increasing population as suggested by the Economic Committee of the Royal Commission on Population, 1950? (6)

7. Comment on the suggestion of the Phillips Committee Report that the age at which National Insurance retirement pensions could be claimed should be raised. (7)

8. What is a major danger of population expansion? (8)

9. What changes in the distribution of population have occurred in Britain since the eighteenth century? (9)

10. What are the present facts about immigrants in Britain? (10, 11)

11. What are the features of the present housing problem? (12)

12. What attempts in town planning have been made during the twentieth century? (13)

13. What are the sociological problems connected with the establishment of new towns? (13)

CHAPTER XVI

CONCLUSION

1. The broad pattern of social development. The general
survey of the social structure which has been made in this
book may point to some pessimistic conclusions: in particular,
the conclusion that in Britain and other European industrialised societies and in the U.S.A. the wrong turn was
taken in the nineteenth century, when the new material
powers available provided a tremendous opportunity to raise
the standard of living and build a new world of plenty and
progress; the opportunities presented by the new technology
were frustrated by human greed and selfishness on the part
of the smart and go-ahead, and by the ignorance, stupidity,
apathy and sheer helplessness of the exploited.

It is evident that exploitation of resources has created
problems of pollution, urban congestion and destruction of
the countryside, with strands of moral and religious processes
having their effects on the family, the structure of social
classes, and the patterns of social values and behaviour.

It is not difficult to trace comparisons with the social
structures of Greece and Rome before their collapse.

2. The transience of change. Nevertheless, it is equally
clear that rapid development has been made in many ways,
producing social stability and progress in the more equitable
distribution of wealth, in the fight against poverty, in education and in the search for a sense of proportion in ordering
human affairs. Changes occur frequently, and a thousand
years is a very short period in the life of humanity. The
social sciences themselves have become recognised disciplines
only during the last hundred years or so, and their existence
is a sign that societies are becoming more aware of themselves.

3. The Social Science Research Council. In 1963 the
Government set up a Committee on Social Studies under the
chairmanship of Lord Heyworth "to review the research being

done in the field of social studies in Government departments, universities and other institutions, and to advise whether changes are needed in the arrangements for supporting and co-ordinating this research." The Report of the Committee was published in June 1965 (Cmnd. 2660); its recommended the establishment of a Social Science Research Council and the expenditure of increased government funds on social research.

In January 1971 the Social Science Research Council announced a five-year grant of £75,000 to the Science Policy Research unit at Sussex University for investigation into forecasting studies, particularly in relation to research and development in industrial and governmental projects.

4. The role of sociology. It may well be that the role of sociology as a co-ordinating discipline will be more defined and less academic than it is at present, less a collection of studies and more a directing and controlling science. "The science of society" will then be worthy of its name.

BIBLIOGRAPHY

It is evident from the text of this **HANDBOOK** that the student of sociology has to read widely. The flood of works on sociological subjects is apt to daunt the beginner, particularly since all the books will probably have a long list of works consulted and recommended. It is a good plan first to look up the various references given in the course of this **HANDBOOK**, then to settle down to a course of reading which, if it at first does not seem to cover a wide field, will give the student a good grounding from which he can proceed with confidence to the study of aspects of social life in which he is most interested.

The following is given as a list of recently published books representative of the kind of reading which the student should pursue. The latest available editions should always be obtained.

General sociology

Stephen Cotgrove, *The Science of Society: An Introduction to Sociology* (Allen and Unwin, 1967).

T. R. Fyvel (ed.), *The Frontiers of Sociology* (Six essays based on B.B.C. Third Programme talks (Routledge and Kegan Paul, 1969)).

Kingsley Davis, *Human Society* (Macmillan, 1949).

G. Duncan Mitchell (ed.), *A Dictionary of Sociology* (Routledge and Kegan Paul, 1968).

Methods

Peter H. Mann, *Methods of Sociological Enquiry* (Basil Blackwell, 1968).

Surveys

Margaret Stacey, *Tradition and Change: A Study of Banbury* (Oxford University Press, 1960).

Peter Willmott, *The Evolution of a Community: A Study of Dagenham* (Routledge and Kegan Paul, 1963).

Colin Rosser and Christopher Harris, *The Family and Social Change: A Study of Family and Kinship in a South Wales Town* (Routledge and Kegan Paul, 1965).

Robert McKenzie and Allan Silver, *Angels in Marble* (Heinemann, 1968).

Social structure

E. A. Johns, *The Social Structure of Modern Britain* (Pergamon Press, 1965).

David C. Marsh, *The Changing Social Structure of England and Wales, 1871–1961* (Routledge and Kegan Paul, 1965).

A. M. Carr-Saunders, D. Caradog Jones and C. A. Moser, *A Survey of Social Conditions in England and Wales, as Illustrated by Statistics* (Oxford University Press, 1965).

The family

Colin Rosser and Christopher Harris, *The Family and Social Change: A Study of Family and Kinship in a South Wales Town* (Routledge and Kegan Paul, 1965).

Christopher Turner, *Family and Kinship in Modern Britain* (Routledge and Kegan Paul, 1969).

Social classes and social mobility

T. B. Bottomore, *Classes in Modern Society* (Allen and Unwin, 1969).

Carole Owen, *Social Stratification* (Routledge and Kegan Paul, 1968).

Colin R. Bell, *Middle-class Families: Social and Geographical Mobility* (Routledge and Kegan Paul, 1969).

D. V. Glass (ed.), *Social Mobility in Great Britain* (Routledge and Kegan Paul, fourth impression, 1967).

The economic background

F. J. Wright, *The Evolution of Modern Industrial Organisation* (Macdonald & Evans, Third Edition, 1967).

Vance Packard, *The Hidden Persuaders* (Penguin Books, 1967).

Political background

F. J. Wright, *British Constitution and Government* (The HANDBOOK Series, Macdonald & Evans, Second Edition, 1973).

H. V. Wiseman, *Political Systems* (Routledge and Kegan Paul, 1966).

The social services

F. J. Wright, *British Social Services* (The HANDBOOK Series, Macdonald and Evans, 1967).

Communications

Alan Hancock, *Mass Communication* (Longmans, Green and Co., 1968).

Crime and youth

T. R. Fyvel, *The Insecure Offenders: Rebellious Youth in the Welfare State* (Penguin Books, 1963).

EXAMINATION TECHNIQUE

A GLANCE at the Test Paper in Appendix III might give a first impression that sociology is a subject in which it is pretty safe to "waffle." This is a dangerous attitude for the candidate to adopt. If the student has read the text of this book carefully he will have realised that although precise information on some matters may be lacking, that is all the more reason why the writer on sociological matters should pick his steps carefully. Hence the frequent use of "it would seem" or "it would appear" in this book. A phrase like "it would appear" should not be an introduction to the free use of the candidate's imagination: the grounds on which a conclusion is reached should be carefully stated. Still less should a sociology paper be regarded as an opportunity to express one's prejudices or convictions.

1. Preparation for an examination.

(a) The candidate should have an adequate *knowledge* of the basic *facts* relating to a particular topic, *e.g.* the family, crime.

(b) He should have done some *reading* on the subject and so be acquainted with different *interpretations* of the facts by various writers.

(c) He should have arrived at some *general conclusions* for himself, and be prepared to support his conclusions by arguments derived from disinterested observation and deduction—a counsel of perfection, for the reasons given in I, 8 (b). Chapter I, 9 may also be read with profit.

(d) Particular *interest* in a topic, such as the family, or religion, or social classes, is an excellent mental attitude, so long as a special effort is made to achieve scientific detachment.

(e) A scrutiny *of past papers* to see the kind of question asked and the scope of the answers expected is a useful and indeed necessary exercise, but the time spent in minute analysis of past questions and forecasting future questions would be better spent in finding out as much information as possible on the major topics dealt with in any paper on sociology.

2. Procedure at the examination.

(a) *Read the whole paper through.* This will enable the

student to gain an impression of the general scope of the paper and of the topics for discussion, and set the brain working on the field of knowledge of the paper.

(b) *Choose the questions you can answer best.* This may seem superfluous advice, but it is amazing how some candidates, put off by some turn of phrase of the examiner or by misunderstanding the examiner's intention, will heave a sigh and regretfully reject a question because it is not phrased just in the way they would have liked it. No examiner is going to ask: "Write all you know about. . . ." He will set a specific problem, probably prefacing it with a request for specific information relating to the problem. He will not expect you to be able to give a definitive and authoritative answer—if you could, you would be the premier Professor of Sociology, and be setting examination papers yourself.

(c) *Read the question* you have chosen; that is, make sure that you realise its demands and its implications. Question 4 in the Test Paper, for example, wants to know if the concept of social classes is justified at all. To answer that, you have to examine the bases on which classifications of social classes have been attempted (not forgetting to suggest what a social class *is*), and suggest whether any classification is justified. Present evidence for this justification.

(d) *Make an outline* of the points you are going to make. This includes headings and sub-headings. You can do this in pencil at the back of your answer book, crossing it out afterwards (the examiner does not want to read any more than is necessary) or on a separate sheet.

  (i) *Check* the outline for irrelevancies and digressions.

  (ii) Ideas relating to the answering of *other questions* will probably come into your mind. Write them down separately for subsequent reference.

(e) *Write* your answer *based on the outline plan.* The student must constantly *refer* to the exact terms of the *question* to make sure he is not straying from the point.

  (i) Plunge into your first point *at once.* Do not waste time and test the examiner's patience by a lengthy introduction; *e.g.* "The question of the family is one of the most important of modern times. Much has been written on the family."

  (ii) See that you have quoted authorities correctly, particularly titles of reports or White Papers and similar official documents. If you have forgotten a title or a date, do not invent a title: "A recent Government White Paper on . . ." is sufficient.

  (iii) In your final paragraph make a *summary* of what

you have said: "It may be concluded, therefore, that . . .": return to the terms of the question and show that you have answered it.

(*f*) *Follow the same procedure* with the other answers. Check that you are not, in your enthusiasm, answering more than the number of questions you are required to answer—you will not earn extra marks.

(*g*) *Check the final script* for errors, mis-spellings and ambiguities. Corrections should be done neatly. Additional points omitted on first writing can be added at the bottom of the answer (leave a little space at the end of each), with an asterisk corresponding to that inserted in the script.

3. Use of English. The English language is a beautiful one. Do not maul it.

(*a*) Avoid clichés and phrases which are in popular use to save looking for the exact statement: "escalate," "spelling it out," "viable," "at this stage" (used merely as an evasion), "expense-wise," etc. Objection to the current use of "this" as a pronoun instead of a demonstrative adjective ("this is true") is probably pedantic, but when used indiscriminately the expression is irritating, as is the constant repetition of, for example, "due to" (for "owing to" or "as a result of").

(*b*) Write *impersonally*, avoiding, for example, "I consider that" or "in my opinion" and do not use *you:* "You can get the same kind of result by. . . ." If the examiner asks for your opinion, he does not expect a cosy chat: say, "the conclusion must be" or "it would appear that," and instead of writing "you can do it another way" use some such phrase as "the same conclusion can be arrived at by. . . ."

4. Prejudice. Everybody has prejudices, and everybody thinks he is something of a sociologist—he is probably right, if he has lived and thought at all. But do not expound your own prejudices the expression "social classes" antagonises many people and, equally, the subject of the House of Lords. If you feel strongly about a topic, *avoid* it—your judgment cannot be trusted. Find another question which you can discuss without heat. Even if you have strong feelings about, say, thuggery, it is better, in an examination answer, to speak about violence with cool detachment, and not go into details, say, about banging old ladies about with heavy instruments.

Sociology as a study is full of pitfalls. One can but try to pick one's way among them.

TEST PAPER

THE following Test Paper is on the lines of the Associated Examining Board Advanced Level Papers. The student should attempt this Test Paper, allowing himself three hours in which to answer five questions, then read through the Examination Technique (Appendix II), then try again and compare the two sets of answers. In this way he can see how his former answers can be improved. Practice along these lines, with reference to the text of this HANDBOOK and to the works listed in the Bibliography, should enable him to face an examination paper with confidence.

Answer *five* questions. *Three* hours allowed.

1. Of what value to the student of sociology is the study of theories of society such as those put forward by, for example, Talcott Parsons and Robert Merton? Make reference to specific issues.

2. Examine the methods used in sociological investigation, and comment on their efficacy.

3. *Either:* (*a*) Account for the changes that have been taking place in family structure in Britain during the twentieth century.
Or: (*b*) Comment on the changed position of married women in the twentieth century.

4. "The concept of social classes nowadays is something of a fiction." Comment.

5. Examine the effect of technological developments on the educational structure of Britain.

6. "Religion is no longer a form of social control in the Western world." Would you agree with this statement? If you think it is true in substance, consider what form of social control related to moral standards could take the place of organised religion.

7. The following table, from the *Monthly Abstract of Statistics,*

March 1973, shows the age distribution of the population of the U.K. in June 1972:

	Nearest '000
All ages	55,789,000
0–14	13,507,000
15–64	34,953,000
65 and over	7,328,000

(*a*) What changes have occurred in the total population during the present century?

(*b*) What changes have occurred in the proportion of the people of working age since 1950?

(*c*) What, on the basis of present trends, are the likely changes in the total and in these age proportions during the next thirty years?

8. (*a*) What are "pressure groups" in the political structure? Give examples.

(*b*) To what extent is it true to say that political parties are pressure groups?

9. What kinds of conflicts arise in individuals and in society as a whole when young persons have to "go out to work"?

10. What light can sociology throw on the apparent fact that crime occurs frequently among young males?

11. "The bureaucrat, like government itself, is a necessary evil in a modern society." Comment.

12. Consider the place in sociological theory and their value in applied sociology of *two* of the following:

(*a*) The concepts of role and status.
(*b*) Functionalism.
(*c*) "Anomie."
(*d*) "Ideal types."

INDEX

163